Lost Mines
and
Buried Treasures
of
Missouri

W.C. JAMESON

NASHVILLE, TENNESSEE

Goldminds Publishing, LLC.
1050 Glenbrook Way, Suite 480
Hendersonville, TN 37075

Lost Mines and Buried Treasures of Missouri

Copyright © W.C. Jameson, October 2011.

Second Edition
ISBN 13: 978-1-930584-61-7

Cover photo copyright © Ron McGinnis, www.ronmcginnis.com

Author photo copyright © Joe Smith

Printed in the United States of America

www.goldmindspub.com

Table of Contents

4/5/1

GS/Nov
8/2017

Introduction

When it comes to tales of famous lost mines and buried treasures, most people don't immediately think of Missouri. The first to come to mind for many are the lost pirate treasures so common along the Atlantic coast or the famous yet elusive Lost Dutchman Mine in the Superstition Mountains of Arizona. As far as the state of Missouri is concerned, this is bad news and good news.

The bad news is that, because of the popularity of so many of the better known tales of lost treasures, the Show Me State has not assumed its rightful position in the world of lore and legend. The truth is, Missouri is quite rich in exciting history and folklore, and it is long past time for the rest of the world to know about this.

The good news is that, unlike other more well known locations for lost mines and buried treasures, Missouri has not been the focus of many searches. Indeed, real and potential sites for hidden caches and forgotten gold and silver mines are rarely visited and have not been picked over. In fact, the opportunities for locating many of these lost treasures are probably as great, or greater, in Missouri than in many other places.

This volume contains twenty-two of some of the most provocative and promising tales of lost mines and buried treasures in Missouri. Many of these stories have been handed down over the generations. Others have been located in old diaries, journals, archives, and via interviews. A few have long been part of Missouri's historical heritage. Just like the abundant folklore and legend related to ghosts and spirits, monsters and madmen, outlaws and cowboys, these tales are part and parcel of the state's culture.

The lure of lost mines and buried treasures has been a fundamental part of human culture since the beginning of time. Who has not thrilled to the quest of Jason and the Argonauts for the golden fleece? Who has not been captivated by the tales of King Solomon's Mines, the Lost Templar Treasure, and so many others. Some of our most popular and enduring literature is involved with the search for lost treasure, as are many popular films and television shows.

In Missouri, the treasures are there. In most cases, records substantiate their existence, but they have remained lost. Because so few know about them, your chances of finding one or more are enhanced. May the pages of this book serve as a suitable beginning for your quest.

Remit, plus hire
Miners + best new mining
machinery — tunneling
Machines?

The Fourteenth Chamber

One of the most compelling tales of lost treasure in the
Missouri Ozarks is the one referred to as the Lost Spanish
Treasure Cave. This legendary cache, consisting of gold
and silver ingots and coins, is located four miles north of
Reeds Spring in Stone County. All of the available research
on this lost treasure points to the fact that it is still there,
however, a number of cave-ins have modified the interior
passageways and closed off access to some of the
chambers.

During the 1960s, an entrepreneur opened a portion of
the cave to tourists, advertising it as an "authentic Spanish
treasure cave." The few who would drive the short distance
from Highway 65 in response to the billboards were given
the opportunity to walk around a small portion of the cave
that was not much different from hundreds of others in the
Missouri Ozarks. Few who visited the cave during the time

it was open knew that it once served as the focus of one of the most intensive treasure hunts ever conducted in the Ozark Mountains.

The existence of the treasure became known in 1888. One day in that year, an old man identified as a Spaniard, arrived in Joplin in search of work. He walked with a stoop, his clothes were old and ragged, his shoes falling apart, and he could barely speak English. In a few days, he was hired by the owner of a local tavern to mop out the place after closing. In exchange, the old man was given some coins and allowed to sleep in a drafty wooden shed behind the place of business.

The Spaniard had been employed for only a few weeks when he became seriously ill. He was taken to the town's only doctor and diagnosed as suffering from tuberculosis but was unable to afford treatment. Two Joplin residents and regular patrons of the tavern where the old man worked took pity on him. They brought him to their room in a nearby hotel and attempted to nurse him back to health. In spite of their efforts, he grew worse.

Once again the physician was summoned. After re-examining the old man, the doctor determined he was dying. He told the two caregivers that the Spaniard had but a short time left to live, then he left.

When the old man learned he would soon die, he asked to speak to his two new friends. He pointed to the pile of his few belongings that had been placed in the corner of the room and told the two men that, in gratitude for their care, he wanted them to have his money and possessions. They thanked him, but were certain the old man possessed little of worth. They sat with him throughout the night, but by dawn he was dead.

After they had carried the body of the Spaniard to the office of the town's undertaker, they returned to their room and gathered up his belongings. Since they consisted of little more than rags, their intention was to burn them. In the pockets were found a few coins which they intended to pass on to the undertaker.

As the two men picked up the clothes, one of them detected something unusual that had been hidden in the lining. After cutting a slit in the fabric with a penknife, he removed a parchment. It was unrolled, placed on a nearby table, and examined closely. It was a map replete with notations, signs, and legends, all in Spanish. Applying what little knowledge of the language they knew, the two men interpreted it as a treasure map, complete with a narrative of how the rich cache came to be hidden in a nearby cave. The year noted on the map was 1522.

According to the document, a party of Spanish soldiers and laborers under the command of one of Hernando de Soto's officers arrived in the Ozarks sometime during the sixteenth century with twenty mule loads of gold and silver ingots. The ore had been mined and processed at some undetermined location in Texas. It was being transported to a location along the Mississippi River where it was to be placed onto flatboats, floated to the Gulf of Mexico, loaded onto a sailing vessel, and shipped across the Atlantic Ocean to Spain to be deposited in that country's treasury.

During the passage through the Ozark Mountains, the Spaniards were victims of numerous attacks by Indians. In spite of the ongoing threat, they searched for signs of more gold and silver. During an extended layover in what is today southwestern Missouri, the Spaniards discovered a vein of silver. The leader of the group gave orders to begin mining immediately. He ordered some of the workers to busy themselves with the construction of a log cabin and a makeshift log fort near the base of an overhanging limestone bluff as protection against the oncoming winter and marauding Indians.

The mining of the silver proceeded without difficulty, but attacks from Indians became a daily hazard. With the passage of several months and the deaths of a number of the soldiers and laborers, the leader decided to abandon the area and return when it was safe to do so. In addition to losing men to the Indians, the Spaniards also had most of their horses and mules stolen. Realizing they did not have the capacity to transport all of their gold and silver, they decided to hide it. Before departing the Ozarks, they carried the ingots deep into a nearby cave and stacked them in one of the many chambers they found there. They covered the entrance and slashed some signs in nearby trees to mark the location. They planned to return and retrieve the treasure at a later time. They were never seen again, and it was presumed they met their fate at the hands of the Indians.

The old Spaniard was given a pauper's burial at the far end of the town's cemetery. Several weeks after he had been interred, the two men who had befriended him, using the old parchment map, decided to undertake a search for the cave containing the cache of ingots. According to the map, it was located in a remote part of Stone County. The directions stated that the search must begin where three trees were arranged in a triangle. Upon the trunk of each of these trees, the Spaniards had carved crescent-shaped marks. The markings, in turn, collectively pointed to the location of the old log fort at the base of an overhanging bluff. Not far from the fort and cabins and along the base of the same bluff was the entrance to the cave.

4

According to the legend on the map, the entrance to the cave had been concealed and disguised to look much like the surrounding area. It was described as low and narrow. To gain access to it, one had to overcome a barrier. After only a few feet of crawling through the opening, the passageway was large enough to allow a man to stand. The passageway extended deep into the bluff for nearly a half-mile to the chamber where the ingots had been stacked. As they proceeded down the passageway, they would pass thirteen chambers. The treasure was in the fourteenth.

For days, the two men searched for the three trees with the crescent-shaped blazes but could never find them. They were forced to return to town when they ran out of provisions. When they could find the time between jobs and other activities, the two friends renewed their hunt for the trees. After two years of searching and finding nothing, they decided to give up. They declared the map a hoax and gave it to a man who worked for the Webb City newspaper. In 1890, an edition of the paper was released with the map printed on a full page.

A few months later, a man named J.J. Mease came into possession of a copy of the newspaper with the map. Mease was a resident of Stone County, Missouri, and had some experience with gold. He had traveled to California during the time of great Gold Rush. Though he had some success working the placer streams of the Sierra Nevada Mountains, he never realized his dreams of becoming wealthy. He decided to return home to the Missouri Ozarks, but he never gave up on the notion of someday finding enough gold to make himself a rich man.

Mease had searched throughout the Ozark Mountains for years for signs of gold and silver. Though he located some outcrops from time to time and sunk some shafts, the veins were exhausted before they yielded any significant return.

Because Mease had spent months prospecting throughout Stone County, he was familiar with the region depicted on the old map. After examining the newspaper copy closely, he decided he could find the location of the treasure cave with little difficulty. After enlisting the help of a long time friend named H.R. Brewer, Mease began preparations to set out in search of the cave.

One afternoon during July in 1894, Mease and Brewer found the three trees arranged in a triangle and containing the crescent-shaped markings on the trunks. Following the directional information interpreted from the blazes, they soon came to a high, overhanging limestone bluff. Near one end they found several large logs in an advanced state of the decay and decided they were once part of the old fort. The location, determined Mease, would have provided significant protection from the weather and was relatively defensible against possible Indian attack. Nearby, they found springs of cool, clear water.

Although they searched the face of the bluff for a full day, they could find no evidence of a cave entrance. Mease and Brewer were confused: They had followed the directions to the letter but were unable to locate their intended target. They rechecked the map several times, and each time they determined it led to this point.

Mease and Brewer employed several nearby residents to help them with their search. Before long, a dozen men were combing the area looking for some sign of a cavern entrance. One of those helping with the search was Mease's young son, Frank.

On the afternoon of the fourth day, one of the men, H.O. Bruffet, was idly digging in the soil not far from the face of the bluff at a location that had been searched several times earlier. At one foot below the surface, Bruffet unearthed a copper bowl. He immediately summoned the others. Mease cleaned the dirt from the bowl and examined it closely. On the surface were a number of Spanish symbols similar to the ones on the map.

Mease encouraged the men to begin digging in this area in hopes of finding more artifacts and evidence. After removing approximately three feet of dirt from an area several square yards in extent, they made an exciting discovery. Beneath the dirt and forest debris that had covered it for centuries were the remains of the fort and its cabins. More importantly, they encountered a large flat limestone slab positioned vertically against the base of the cliff. Upon the face of the slab were incised several symbols like those found on the map and the bowl.

During the search, it never occurred to Mease that the entrance to the Spanish treasure cave might lay below the surface of the ground they were searching. As a result of hundreds of years of deposition and accumulation of rock, soil, and forest debris, the level of the ground became higher than the entrance to the cave.

Attempts to remove the large stone failed, so the men attacked it with hammers and broke it up. Once the smaller pieces were removed, a low, narrow opening was exposed. To enter the cave, a man had to slither along on his belly. The opening and first few feet of the passageway soon enlarged enough such that one could crawl through. After several yards, there was enough room to stand.

Just inside the entrance were piles of ash and charcoal, suggesting human use and occupation at one time. Several yards beyond the ashes, the floor of the passageway dropped abruptly for twelve feet, necessitating the use of a rope to reach the lower level. At that point, it straightened out again. At the bottom of the slope Mease found the skeletons of three men. Lying alongside the skeletons were odd pieces of metal he determined were parts of Spanish armor.

Also discovered among the bones was a mold made of porcelain. The mold was described as being six inches deep and two-and-a-half feet long. Aside from its large size, it appeared to be a mold used to form ingots. The resulting bars would have been unusually long and very heavy. Mease began to have doubts. When he inspected the inside of the mold, however, he discovered it was coated with a thin film of silver.

As Mease examined the mold, several of the workers explored the passageway. Not far from the skeletons, they found more Spanish inscriptions scratched onto one side of the cavern wall. The inscriptions were similar to the ones they had seen on the stone slab.

Mease was convinced this was the Spanish treasure cave. Along with Brewer, he formed a company to include the workers. Together, they would remove the cache of gold and silver ingots and split the profit equally. One of the laborers, a man named C.C. Bush, offered to ride to Galena, the nearest large settlement, and obtain a formal deed to the land on which the cave was located. As he was filling out paperwork pertinent to applying for the deed, Bush learned that the land in question was already owned by the Frisco Railway. Following several days of negotiations, the railroad company agreed to sell it to Mease's company for three dollars an acre. All of the men contributed equally and ultimately purchased several acres of the land surrounding the cave.

A few days following the purchase, Mease and his company arrived at the site and began clearing away debris and enlarging the opening of the cave. They established a camp nearby where they took their meals and slept in tents. On the evening of the second day of work, a young man arrived at the camp and asked a number of questions about the digging and clearing. He was directed to Mease.

Mease found the stranger ill-equipped to be traveling in such rugged Ozark country. He was tall, well-groomed, and dressed in an expensively tailored suit in the manner of a successful attorney. His skin was olive-colored and he spoke with a Spanish accent. He said he had arrived in the area days earlier and was querying area residents about the cave. Eventually, they directed him to Mease's campsite.

Following some small talk, the newcomer came to the point of his visit. He made Mease an offer of one thousand dollars for the deed to the land on which the excavation was taking place. Mease excused himself and conferred for several minutes with the rest of the company. He returned to the stranger and informed him they were rejecting his offer. The Spaniard thanked Mease for his time and departed.

Mease and his friends believed they were on the verge of recovering the long-lost Spanish treasure, and the appearance of the young Spaniard, along with his offer of a significant amount of money, convinced them even more that something of value was lying within the cave.

Two days later, the well-dressed Spaniard returned. He asked permission to observe the progress associated with the excavation. Mease invited him to remain with them and had an extra tent set up for the visitor. As the days passed, Mease and the Spaniard became friends, both keenly interested in the outcome of the search.

Following his first few days in the camp, the Spaniard told Mease he had something to show him. He produced an ancient map similar to the one Mease encountered in the Webb City newspaper. This map carried even more detail than the first. It contained a detailed narrative of the twenty mule loads of gold and silver, the fourteen chambers to be found inside the cave, and the stacking of the ingots in the last chamber. It also described the discovery of a rich vein of silver found not far away, one that yielded almost pure ore that was mined and smelted by DeSoto's men nearly four hundred years earlier.

The Spaniard continued to make offers to Mease, and even attempted to become one of the partners, but when Mease discussed it with his company, they refused the newcomer's involvement. Following the latest rejection, the Spaniard packed his belongings, bade Mease goodbye, and rode away. He was never seen again.

The opening of the cave had finally been enlarged enough that men could enter and leave with little difficulty. Furthermore, the steep drop had been leveled, allowing for easier movement. One morning, the company, carrying digging tools, torches and lanterns entered the cave, certain that by the end of the day they would all be wealthy men. Because the son, Frank Mease, was only eight years old, he was not permitted to accompany the workers. He remained behind in camp.

They had been in the cave no more than ten minutes when they began to encounter problems. The floor was difficult to impossible to traverse. During the years since the Spaniards had hidden their gold and silver, large rocks had fallen from the oft-fractured roof, piling up on the floor. In some cases, climbing over the obstacles was laborious and dangerous. In other cases, passage was blocked and the rocks had to be broken up and carried out of the cave.

Water dripped continuously from the ceiling. As a result, the floor was muddy and slippery. They worked a total of fourteen hours that first day, and only succeeded in penetrating thirty yards of the cave.

As they made their way deeper into the cavern, the men encountered more sudden drops and rises as well as more rock-choked passages. Progress was slow, sometimes only a few feet per day. By the end of the first week, they had encountered three of the fourteen chambers. One of the workers fell while attempting to cross a pile of boulders and broke his leg. Because of the difficult passage, it took a full day to carry the man out.

The next morning as they entered the cave, they carried enough torches and provisions to last forty-eight hours. With the goal of untold wealth awaiting them at the end of their quest, enthusiasm remained undiminished. This time, young Frank Mease was allowed to accompany the workers. He was given a shovel and told he was expected to work as hard as the others. He participated with zeal. The recent experiences in the cave caused the men to proceed with greater caution as they were concerned with what new obstacles they might encounter this day.

The days turned into weeks. Onward they pushed – crawling, climbing, and sliding over, under, and around obstacles. More injuries occurred, none of them serious, but enough to delay progress as men were carried out of the cavern. More cave-ins were encountered, many of them, Mease deduced, were recent. After examining the limestone closely, he found it to be very brittle with thin layers. Furthermore, he told his men, earthquakes over the past four hundred years had weakened the rock. He cautioned them to take care.

More time passed, and they finally came to the thirteenth chamber. Spurred on by the anticipation of the gold and silver that lay just beyond, they crawled forward only to encounter their greatest disappointment thus far.

When they arrived at what would have been the fourteenth chamber, they found it had been effectively sealed by a huge cave-in. Thousands of tons of rock and debris blocked the entrance. Furthermore, at this point, the passageway was so low and narrow that it precluded wielding a heavy hammer to break up the rock.

In spite of the obvious difficulty in entering the fourteenth chamber, Mease encouraged the men to dig into the rubble as best they could. Armed with shovels and picks they attempted to make headway, but it soon became clear their efforts were futile. The mass of rock that lay between them and treasure would take months, likely years, to remove by hand. Discouraged, the company returned to the outside to nurse their disappointment.

Following two days of discussions, Mease and his followers decided that whatever treasure might lie between them and the tons of rock blocking entrance to the fourteenth chamber was not worth the effort or expense it would take to retrieve it. The company was disbanded, and the men returned to their farms, businesses, and families.

The dream of reaching the treasure of gold and silver ingots did not die with Mease's abandonment of the project. As much or more as the others, Frank was disappointed when it was announced that the search for the lost treasure cache was to be discontinued. Like his father so many years before, his son, Frank, nurtured a dream of finding the treasure. Now in his twenties, his dream grew stronger with each day. He came to believe that he would be the one to break through the obstacles and enter the fourteenth chamber.

Frank decided on a different approach to the task of reaching the treasure. He determined that the job could be pursued more efficiently if the workers were not encumbered with torches and lanterns. Frank recalled that here and there throughout the cavern was a swiftly running stream. Using the energy of the flowing water, he constructed a flume that directed the stream to a location where he installed a water wheel. The flowing water would turn the wheel which in turn would activate a generator that powered the lights.

After installing lights in the cave up to the fourteenth chamber, Frank then examined the possibilities of using the flowing water to carry away some of the smaller rock and dirt that blocked the entrance. As he was working on a way to accomplish this, another cave-in occurred. A large portion of the cavern roof gave way, and thousands of tons of rock collapsed to the floor of the cave blocking passage beyond the third chamber.

With the cave-in, the months of planning and work had been negated. After a close examination of the disaster, Frank determined it would be impossible to penetrate the new obstacle.

Because he had so much time, energy, and money invested in this project, Frank decided to try to salvage some of it. Having a flair for enterprise, he was determined to make the best of an unfortunate situation. He had a road graded from Highway 65 to a location close to the cave entrance. Along the highway, he constructed billboards which advertised the "Lost Spanish Treasure Cave" and charged tourists a small admission fee. They would gather at the cave entrance, and Frank would relate the story of the lost treasure and the attempts to retrieve it.

Following a thorough analysis of the existing documentation, along with a consideration of the great investment of time, money, and labor of many men, there appears to be little doubt that a great treasure in gold and silver ingots lies hidden deep in the fourteenth chamber of the old cave. Experts on caverns in the Ozark Mountains claim this cave may have passageways that run for miles underground, and that they may be connected to other caves in the area. They have suggested that it may be possible to reach the fourteenth chamber via another below-ground route.

In recent years, a group of engineers has proposed sinking a vertical shaft from some point on top of the bluff into the fourteenth chamber, but thus far its exact location has not been determined.

Some old-timers who live in the area have suggested that when the Spaniards abandoned the area in the sixteenth century, they placed a curse on the treasure cave. They point out the number of men who have been injured and the continuous obstacles that have prevented them from reaching the treasure. They claim that only the rightful heirs to the fortune in the cave will be able to retrieve it.

Still, men continue to arrive in this area from around the country and continue to seek ways to reach the fourteenth chamber.

[handwritten notes, top of page:] Also, try to find names & property addresses of skeleton find in '30s and farmer plowing field (pp 22 & 23, resp)

[handwritten, top right:] Drag a mat antenna back and forth w/ a 4 wheeler in every bluff in those areas.

[handwritten:] GS

[handwritten:] Find out closest spot to do online research re: this story, and keep in mind potential of river alteration (see pg. 21) Then

Lost Kettle of Gold Coins near the Missouri River

[handwritten annotation:] Base or Cave or deep bluff narrows it to a 2-D.

The northern portions of the Ozark Mountains are unlike *[or]* the rugged, dissected uplands found in southwestern *[nearly]* Missouri and northwestern Arkansas. Here there are no *[So.]* deep valleys, narrow hollows, and high ridges so common *[com]* farther south and so often associated with this range. *[at]* Instead, one finds a series of undulating hills rising *[parallel to]* gradually from the Missouri River Valley. Here and there *[bluffs]* some of them have been eroded into steep-sided bluffs. *[could]* Level patches of prairie, floodplain, and farms are *[natural]* common. *[it]*

Farming the floodplain of the Missouri River has proven *[Imme]* productive and profitable over the generations. The rich, *[ly]* dark alluvial soils, along with abundant rainfall, yield *[%]* healthy crops. At places along the floodplain, exposed *[then]* limestone bluffs can be found, having been carved and *[one]* shaped as the river continued its downward erosion for *[at]* millennia. Some of these exposed bluffs extend almost to *[right]* the banks of the river. Near one of them, four French *[right]* traders buried a copper kettle filled to the top with gold *[angles.]*

coins. The year was 1802. The coins have never been found.

St. Louis was the last settlement of any consequence encountered by trappers, traders, entrepreneurs, and adventurers setting out to brave the uncharted wilderness of the West. Few knew what lay beyond, and rumor and lore of the real and potential dangers that might be encountered were rampant. To venture beyond St. Louis was a bold undertaking. Many traveled westward up the Missouri River. Along the great stream could be found trading posts, tiny settlements, and streams full of beaver whose pelts brought high prices in the east. In addition, Indian campgrounds were often encountered along the river. Some of the tribes were friendly to the travelers, but most were not.

Trading posts had been established at the confluence of the Missouri and other significant rivers. These included the Kaw, Republican, and Platte. It was to these trading posts that trappers living in far-flung regions farther to the west would bring their pelts each year to trade for supplies and equipment, or to sell for gold.

During certain times of the year, the Missouri River saw high boat traffic as a result of the commerce related to trapping. In addition to bundles of pelts being floated downriver, boats filled with trade goods and containers of gold coins traveled upriver.

During the second week of October, 1802, a small wooden craft made its way up the Missouri. It was rowed by four Frenchmen who were in the employ of a French trading company based out of St. Louis. In addition to being piled high with trade goods, the boat carried a copper kettle filled to the brim with gold coins, all of French origin. In addition to delivering the goods, the principal instruction to the four Frenchmen on departing St. Louis was to guard the gold – with their lives if necessary.

Rowing upstream on the Missouri River was difficult. The Frenchmen had been on their journey for only a few days when they grew tired of the continuous labor. Weary, they were already wishing for an end to the trip. They needed to make haste, however, for it was imperative they delivered the goods and the money and return to St. Louis before the winter storms arrived.

The four Frenchmen rowed for long hours each day against the strong current. Slowly, they made their way upstream. As they rowed, they remained constantly on the alert for hostile Indians known to be in the region. At the end of the day they pulled onto a riverbank and set up camp, always posting a sentry. From time to time they ventured a short distance inland to hunt for game. Only two would go while the other two would remain with the boat and cargo.

Days passed, and the Frenchmen had not seen a single Indian since they began their trip. They grew complacent, and began to suspect the tales they had heard back in St. Louis of wild savages had been exaggerated. Heretofore as they rowed upstream, they scanned the riverbanks for signs of danger. Now they took turns on the oars, with two napping while two rowed.

Early one evening during the second week of their journey, the Frenchmen searched the riverbank for a suitable campsite. On the north side of the river they spotted several low bluffs set back from the bank a few dozen yards. They selected one with an overhang that could protect them from inclement weather. They rowed toward it.

When they were only a few feet from the riverbank, dozens of screaming Indians charged out of a nearby stand of willows on the opposite shore. As the Frenchmen stared in horror, the Indians began firing arrows at them and launching canoes into the river.

As the Indians paddled their crafts across the current, the Frenchmen landed and pulled their own up onto the bank. Seeing that they were outnumbered, they determined they would have to make a stand against their attackers. Grabbing their weapons and a few belongings, they raced about forty yards to the shelter of the nearest bluff where they took up positions behind some rocks. Two of the Frenchmen ran back to the boat to retrieve the heavy kettle filled with gold coins. With difficulty, they carried it to their place of shelter as arrows flew all about them.

As the Frenchmen hastily stacked rocks and driftwood in an attempt to fashion a fortification, the sun was beginning to set and darkness encroached upon their position. In the dim light, they spotted the Indians moving about in the near distance. A musket shot felled one of them and caused the others to scatter for cover.

All during the night, the Frenchmen could see the Indians moving from cover to cover as they sought positions nearer to the bluff. After two hours, they had established themselves in a semi-circle, thus cutting off any escape route from the bluff to the boat. As the night chill set in, small campfires were built where groups of two to three Indians were hunkered down. Throughout the night, the four Frenchmen remained alert for any sign of attack. They were unable to sleep, and they dreaded the approaching dawn.

During the night the temperature dropped dramatically as a cold front passed through the area. Just as the morning sky grew light, an early storm struck. Thick, heavy snowfall reduced visibility to only a few feet and within two hours accumulated on the ground to a depth of nearly twelve inches.

The Frenchmen deduced that the snowstorm interfered with the Indians' plan to attack. During infrequent lulls in the snow fall, they could see their attackers huddled around their fires. Now and then an arrow was fired into the makeshift fortress under the bluff.

In their haste to flee the attacking Indians at the riverbank, the Frenchmen neglected to retrieve any food. During the night, they had burned most of the dry wood they found lying nearby. Their fire had dwindled and it was growing colder. One of them was suffering frostbite and a severe cold and tried to warm himself by the fire.

For four days the Frenchmen remained trapped in their fortification. The one who suffered frostbite died. With their food gone and their firewood depleted, the three remaining decided their only chance for survival was to try to make a break for the boat, launch it into the river, and return to St. Louis.

It was clear they would not be able to transport the heavy copper kettle filled with gold coins. One hour past sunset of the fourth day, they carried the kettle to a location just beyond the shelter of the fortress and buried at the base of the bluff. They felt certain that if they survived the Indians, they would be able to return to this location and retrieve the gold.

The three men waited several more hours until they were certain the Indians were asleep. Excercising great caution, they crept from their fortress and made their way silently toward the boat. When they were still twenty yards from the craft they were spotted by an Indian scout who shouted an alarm.

Simultaneously, the Frenchmen fired their muskets into the oncoming group of attackers, killing two. They turned and raced for the boat. In the few seconds it took to reach the craft, two of the Frenchmen were struck by multiple arrows and fell dead.

Reaching the boat, the survivor shoved with all the strength he could muster and succeeded in launching it into the river. He jumped in, lay down in the bottom of the craft, and let the current carry him downstream. It was at that point that he realized he had been struck by three arrows: two in one leg and another in his side. For reasons unknown, the Indians did not pursue him.

During the night the surviving Frenchman lost a great deal of blood from his wounds. For days he lapsed in and out of consciousness. Near death, he finally arrived in St. Louis. He was lifted from the boat and carried to a physician. His arrow wounds were treated, but the frostbite he endured during the freezing days and nights of his return journey required that his limbs be amputated.

Days later when the Frenchman regained consciousness, he related the story of the attack by the Indians, the deaths of his companions, and the burying of the kettle filled with gold coins. A representative of the fur trading company visited him and listened closely as the Frenchman described in detail the bluff where they had taken shelter and buried the gold. The representative said that with the coming of spring the company would send a party of men to the site to retrieve the cache.

Well into April the weather had warmed, but because of reports of ongoing Indian depredations along the river, no recovery party was ever organized. The trading company decided to wait for at least c̶ ̶o̶n̶ ̶u̶...̶ recover the gold.

Exactly one year later, the trading company organized a party of men to travel to the bluff, retrieve the gold, and return with it to St. Louis. Three days into the expedition, however, every man was struck with dysentery and the party was forced to abandon the search. As the months wore on, the trading company became preoccupied with other aspects of their business, and soon the copper kettle filled with gold coins was forgotten.

In 1835, a large party of French trappers departed St. Louis and traveled by boat up the Missouri River to the rich beaver trapping grounds far to the west. The men, all veterans of the fur trade, were well armed and experienced in warfare with Indians. They traveled in five boats.

For days they rowed upriver, and during that time were never approached by Indians. A few men in the party were familiar with the misfortune of the four Frenchmen in 1802 and the caching of the copper kettle filled with gold coins. They possessed only vague knowledge of the details, but were determined to search for the cache.

One day they spotted some bluffs on the north side of the river that were similar to the ones described by the Frenchman who hid the gold. Since 1802, the ever-shifting channel of the Missouri River had changed. A flood had caused it to jump its banks and slice a new channel a quarter of a mile north of the old one. In spite of the changes in the alluvial landscape, the trappers decided this was where the gold had been buried. Though they searched the area for several days, they were never able to locate the kettle.

Decades passed, and the streams once abundant with beaver and other fur-bearing animals of the Rocky

Mountains were gradually trapped out. The shrinking supply of pelts, coupled with the lower demand of the belly fur for beaver hats spelled the end for trappers and traders throughout the West.

As a result, human traffic up and down the river diminished to almost nothing. It would remain thus until the end of the Civil War when hopeful settlers began swarming westward across the Mississippi River, up the Missouri, and toward the Rocky Mountains and west coast.

Among the west-bound migrants were many who saw the promise of the fertile alluvial soils along the course of the Missouri River. Several decided to settle there and try their luck at farming in this new and relatively undeveloped country. Not many years passed when settlements sprung up along the river, and area farms began yielding abundant crops. Homesteaders planted on every available patch of the fertile soil right up to the bases of the limestone bluffs that fronted the river.

During the 1930s, some carpenters were constructing the foundation for a new home near the base of one of these bluffs not far from where the Grand River enters the Missouri. As they dug into the soft earth to set some corner stones, they uncovered a skeleton under a low mound of dirt. Among the items found in association with the skeleton was a copper disc bearing the engraved image of the flag of France. Weeks later, it was learned that such discs were issued to their representatives by a French fur trading company once based in St. Louis.

The skeleton was taken to a physician located in the nearest village. Following a thorough examination, he determined that it belonged to a Caucasian and had been underground for more than one hundred years. It was assumed by those familiar with the story that the skeleton was the remains of the Frenchman who had frozen to death during the siege by the Indians in 1802.

The discovery of the skeleton ignited interest in the possibility that the copper kettle filled with gold coins could be found nearby. The cache represented a huge fortune, and searchers came from miles away to try their luck. As it turned out, the tale of the buried treasure was widely known throughout much of the northern Ozark Mountains and had long since entered the realm of folklore.

One day in 1935, an elderly Indian woman arrived in the area and began making inquires about the skeleton that had been found. She wanted to know the precise spot from which it had been disinterred. To those who asked, she explained that her grandfathers had often told her the story of members of the tribe who waged a fight against four Frenchmen who arrived in a boat. She possessed a French coin dated 1799 that she said was taken from the body of one of the slain men. She also claimed to have some knowledge of the buried treasure. For nearly a week she searched along the base of the bluff to which she had been directed. Having no success at finding anything, she left and was never seen again.

In 1941, a Missouri River valley farmer was plowing his field that extended to within thirty yards of a low limestone bluff. A glint of something that had been turned up by the plow caught his eye and he stopped to investigate. It was a gold coin dated 1796 and bore French inscriptions. After showing the coin to several acquaintances, he learned the story of the lost kettle. He returned to the same area several times to search for the cache but could never find it.

The belief that the copper kettle containing the rich treasure of gold coins is still buried near one of the limestone bluffs overlooking the Missouri River is strong among area residents. The people here are proud of their history and lore, and can relate tales of Indians, explorers, early settlement, and buried treasure.

The tales, they will tell the visitor, can be had for the asking. The lost gold coins buried somewhere along the river will be more difficult to obtain. In spite of that, people still arrive in this area to search, ever hopeful of digging up the copper kettle.

65

I've read about this before. The location is unquestionably known.

Private Property - get permission.

Buried Keg of Gold Coins

Barnard, Missouri, is a small, quiet town located on the eastern edge of the Great Plains in Nodaway County in the northwestern part of the state. Only a few people live in Barnard today, and most claim little has changed in this community for several generations.

Just to the west of Barnard is the north-south trending Highway 71. Years ago it was called the Old Stagecoach Road. Near the highway is the site of the former home of the late Dr. Lynn Talbott. The grand house has long since fallen down as a result of neglect, and much of the ground where it once stood overlooking the road has been graded over. The residence was once referred to by old-timers in the area as the House of Seven Gables.

The barn, which was located a short distance from the house, is also gone. At some unknown location between the house and the barn and just a few inches below the surface lies buried an old nail keg filled to the top with gold coins. If found today, this fortune is estimated to be worth in excess of a half-million dollars.

In the first few years following the Civil War, portions of the west and mid-west opened up for settlement. Some who longed to establish farms and create towns and

Near IR Goggles to find

Rem it sins?

businesses were attracted to the region of northwest Missouri. As a result, migration from the eastern states onto the Great Plains followed, a movement that lasted for years.

During this time, Lynn Talbot lived in Connecticut. Talbott was a physician with a successful practice, but watching so many of his neighbors packing their belongings into wagons and heading westward caused him to think about the opportunities that might lie toward the sunset. Having his own need for adventure to satisfy, Talbott longed to visit this unknown country about which he had heard so much.

After consulting with his wife, Mary, and his two sons, Charles and Hugh, Talbott sold his house and practice, packed the family's belongings into two newly purchased wagons, and set out for Barnard, Missouri. Talbott was highly regarded in the community where he practiced medicine, and his patients hated to see him leave. He told them he looked forward to delivering babies, treating disease, and repairing broken bones in his new home on the Great Plains.

Months later, the Talbott family arrived in Barnard. As the only doctor for miles around, he prospered and was soon able to build a large, elegant house overlooking Stagecoach Road northwest of town. Mrs. Talbott saw to the decorating and soon the structure was filled with expensive furnishings, everything she and her husband deemed essential to the comfort and luxury enjoyed by a successful doctor.

During this time, few people trusted banks. As a result of the turmoil created by the Civil War and unstable economic system that followed, along with the constant threat of bank robbers, most tended to take care of their savings in their own way. Many farmers placed money in a coffee can or Mason jar and buried it at some location on their property rather than trust it to a bank.

Talbott was no exception. Because gold was the only thing that held its value during post-Civil War times, he insisted that his fees be paid in that manner. The coins were then placed in a pouch attached to his belt. Each night when he arrived home, he removed the coins from the pouch and dropped them into a nail keg he kept in the hall closet.

After a few years, Dr. Talbott's nail keg was filled to the top with denominations of five, ten, and twenty dollar gold pieces. Sons Charles and Hugh were aware of the coin-filled keg, and later admitted that from time to time they purloined one or two of the coins. Such thefts were small and infrequent and the physician never noticed. As the barrel filled and the fortune increased, however, the two sons, now older and able to appreciate the meaning of money, became desirous of more. Surreptitiously, they made plans to acquire the keg of gold coins. After several weeks of discussions, the two brothers decided to kill their father in order to gain possession of his treasure.

At the same time, Talbott began to grow uncomfortable about having so much money in the house. Without telling his wife or sons, he decided to bury the keg of gold coins. One day after arriving home in the evening, he pretended to be pruning rose bushes in the yard while he secretly selected a suitable location between the house and the barn for his cache. Later that night as his family slept, Talbott crept outside and excavated a shallow hole to accommodate the keg. It required several trips to transport the keg and all of its contents to the site, but after two hours Talbott completed the job. He covered the hole, placed a new keg in the closet, and went to bed. It was 2:00 a.m. on the morning of December 12, 1879.

The next day following dinner, Talbott, as was his custom, retreated to his favorite chair near the hearth. Outside, the snow fell; inside a warm fire blazed. Talbott soon fell asleep. Across the room, a window had been propped open a few inches to allow a bit of fresh air into the room. As Mary Talbott was drying the dishes, she heard what she thought was a gunshot and rushed to the living room. There, she found her husband lying dead in his chair, a bullet hole in his forehead.

Andrew Toel, the county sheriff, lived in the county seat of Maryville, about ten miles away. He was summoned and arrived a few hours later. Toel was a well-respected citizen of Nodaway County and regarded as a competent lawman and reputable investigator. For most of the night, Toel searched throughout the house for clues to the murder. Then he turned his attention to the outside. Near the open window he found footprints, but they were indistinct.

Toel concluded that the doctor had been shot by an unknown assailant standing outside the window, but was unable to find a single substantive clue to the identity of the murderer. During his investigation, Toel harbored an uncomfortable suspicion that Charles and Hugh Talbott knew more about the killing than they let on. Both appeared anxious around the lawman and nervously glanced at one another when being interrogated.

After spending several hours in the Talbott home, Toel told the physician's wife that he would return to Maryville, analyze the information he had gathered, and promised to return to continue the investigation.

By the time Sheriff Toel was out of sight, the two brothers raced to the closet to retrieve the nail keg filled with gold coins. They were shocked to discover only three gold pieces lying at the bottom. Frantically, they searched other closets in the house, but found no trace of the missing keg. When Mrs. Talbott asked her sons why they were behaving in such a strange manner, they explained they were upset as a result of the death of their father.

Three weeks after Dr. Talbott's demise, Mrs. Talbott responded to a knock at the front door. When she opened it, she found a stranger standing on the porch. The man's clothes were old and well-worn, but clean. His appearance was humble and he looked as if he had traveled a great distance. When she asked what she could do for him, the stranger introduced himself as John Chandler. Chandler explained that he had been traveling the countryside in search of work. He said he was very hungry, and was willing to put in a full day of labor for a hot meal. Finding it difficult to turn the poor man away, Mrs. Talbott prepared him a splendid meal and then got him busy splitting firewood and repairing some broken hinges on the barn door. At the invitation of Mrs. Talbott, Chandler spent the night in the barn.

The next morning after feeding Chandler breakfast, Mrs. Talbott complimented him on being a hard worker and offered him permanent employment. The arrangement was agreeable to Charles and Hugh. The brothers were now responsible for managing the Talbott estate which included a large farm, and they welcomed the competent and hard-working Chandler. After a few weeks, the three men became friends.

Chandler was a quiet man, seldom given to talk and kept to himself. When Charles and Hugh attempted to draw him into conversation, Chandler remained polite and attentive, but after a few minutes excused himself and went about his work. He appeared to prefer solitude over company. The brothers noticed that whenever a visitor arrived at the

Talbott home, Chandler would retreat to the barn and remain out of sight until the company departed.

One day while Charles, Hugh, and Chandler were moving cattle from one pasture to another, the brothers asked the hired man why he was so reclusive. Chandler replied that he was hiding from the law because he had killed a man in Tennessee.

The brothers had a good laugh over this. They explained to Chandler that he had nothing to worry about because only a few months earlier they had killed their own father. They told Chandler about the nail keg filled with gold coins and how they were never able to locate it. That night, John Chandler disappeared.

Unknown to the Talbotts, Chandler was a private detective from Kansas City who had been hired by Sheriff Toel to investigate the murder of the physician. After hearing the brothers admit to the killing, Chandler rode to Maryville and informed Toel. Two days later, the sheriff arrived at the Talbott house and arrested Charles and Hugh for the murder of their father. The brothers were tried, found guilty, and sentenced to hang. Following a series of failed appeals, the two men were executed on July 22, 1881.

For years, Mary Talbott wondered about the fate of the nail keg filled with gold coins. She searched the house and the grounds but was never able to find it. Others who heard the story of the physician's buried fortune would arrive at the house and offer to assist Mrs. Talbott in her search. She always refused them.

If found today, the nail keg filled with gold pieces would be worth a substantial fortune. It is a matter of historical documentation that Dr. Talbott buried a nail keg filled with gold coins somewhere on his property. That much is certain. Given what little information is available regarding the location of the cache, it is reasonable to assume it is located in a shallow hole only a few feet from the site of the old Talbott home. If the location of the old house and barn could be determined, a reasonable search area could be delineated. The nail keg filled with gold coins would be found mere inches from the surface. Since this is private property, any search must begin with gaining permission.

print permission
slip/
50%
agreement
and
+
confidentiality
agreement.
(for them
to never
mention
my name
except
where
legally
required)

BLM for old records, or ask them who would have them — county? It was 1881.

then, hire someone who understands how to frame the location given in records to + modern map.
Remember, etc. & Cam-search

The Yoachum Silver Dollars

One of the most famous and enduring tales of lost treasure ever to come out of the Missouri Ozarks concerns what are called "The Yoachum Dollars." That the Yoachum Dollars existed there can be no doubt. A number of collectors have samples, and government records substantiate their existence because they were illegally manufactured coins. The source of the silver used in the making of the illegal dollars, along with the circumstances associated with their manufacture, is still being debated after a century-and-a-half.

This strange tale has its beginnings in 1541. During that time, Spanish explorers under the command of Hernando de Soto's officers penetrated the rugged and remote valleys of the Ozark Mountains in southwestern Missouri. Here and there they found outcrops of ore. The discoveries proved promising enough to generate small settlements while the mines were developed. Near the mouth of James River where it enters the White River, the Spanish constructed a log fortress atop what is called Breadtray Mountain today. The mountain is three miles northwest of the town of Lampe and not far from Table Rock Lake.

Near the fortress, the Spanish discovered several outcrops of silver. A short distance away they found a cave. Evidence found inside suggested it had been used as a shelter for the indigenous residents for centuries. The cave penetrated the mountains, dividing into numerous passageways that, it was estimated, extended for miles.

Once the digging of the ore commenced, several Indians had been captured and enslaved to work in the mines. The ore was removed from the rock matrix, carried to a nearby location where it was processed, melted, and then poured into molds to form eighteen-inch-long ingots. As the ingots accumulated, they were stacked along one wall of the cave's numerous passageways.

When a significant number of ingots had been processed, the Spaniards intended to load them onto burros and transport them to some location on the Mississippi River located far to the east. Here, the ingots would be placed on a raft and floated downriver to the Gulf of Mexico where they would be loaded onto a ship and delivered to the Spanish treasury across the Atlantic Ocean.

The Indian slaves were treated cruelly by the Spaniards. They were forced to work long hours. If they didn't excavate the silver as quickly as their masters wished, they would be subjected to whippings and starvation. It has been told that many of them died in their chains.

From time to time, other Indians were spotted observing the comings and goings at the mine from nearby ridges. They were always well-armed, carrying lances and bows and arrows. Since they appeared menacing, the Spaniards tripled the guard.

Every week, the leader of the Spanish settlement would send out a hunting party to procure game for the pot. These groups were often confronted by Indians, and the confrontations often led to fighting. Several Spaniards were killed during the brief battles. Some hunting parties never returned.

As the number of Spaniards decreased from Indian depredations and as more and more Indians were seen watching from the ridges, the officer in charge began considering the possibility of loading up what silver that had been accumulated and abandoning the mines.

During the next few days as the Spaniards deliberated leaving the area, the Indians launched a vicious attack on the fort and mine at the same time. Hundreds of them streamed out of the woods, shooting, slicing, and hacking the Spaniards until most of them were killed. At the mine, the overseers were overrun and slain and the captives released. A handful of Spaniards escaped, but the ingots of silver ore they had accumulated remained stacked in the cave.

After the Spaniards were driven from the area, the Indians ruled supreme. Two-and-a-half centuries would pass before the region was inhabited by white men again. The silver ingots and the mines remained undisturbed until 1809. In that year, according to Choctaw oral history, a small hunting party arrived in the area and was caught in a sudden, violent storm. In search of immediate shelter, they stumbled into the opening of a large cave. Just inside the entrance, they found several skeletons, no doubt the victims of the Indian attack over 250 years earlier.

As the storm raged for two days, the Choctaws decided to investigate the cave. Using dry limbs and grasses they found in the opening, they fashioned torches and explored the many passageways. In this manner, they chanced upon the stacks of silver ingots in one of the labyrinthine arteries.

As with most Indians, the Choctaw had little use for precious metals save for the occasional fashioning of ornaments. However, they learned that the white settlers in the area placed great value on the gold and silver found in these mountains. As a result, the Indians sometimes traded the ore for provisions, horses, and firearms. For several years following their discovery of the ingots, the Choctaw visited this cave to retrieve just enough silver to make jewelry and conduct trade with the whites. Small groups of Choctaw Indians sometimes traveled as far as St. Louis to purchase goods.

One afternoon, a large group of Mexicans approaching the location of the cave and the mines was spotted by a Choctaw scout. The leader of the tribe was summoned. Along with three warriors, he rode out to meet the newcomers and to inquire about their reasons for entering the Indian homeland.

The leader of the Mexicans explained they had come in search of a silver mine they believed to be in this area. He said the mine was worked by Spaniards generations earlier, and they had hopes of reopening it. The Mexican retrieved a wrapped object from his saddlebags. After removing the protective cover, he unrolled a large sheepskin map that containing Spanish writing and symbols. The Choctaw chieftain recognized nearby prominent landmarks.

Following an intense examination of the map and an extended conversation with the Mexican, the chief told him there was no such mine. He encouraged the Mexicans to depart the area as soon as possible.

The Mexicans rode away, but a Choctaw scout reported that they had set up what appeared to be a permanent camp a short distance away. Fearful that the Mexicans would return and find the mines and the ingots, the chief ordered that the entrances to the shafts and the cave be closed and the area abandoned until it was safe to return. As the legend states, the entrances to the mines were hidden as a result of the Indians creating small landslides on the slopes above them. More rocks and forest debris were reportedly stacked in front of the cave entrance making it look much like the rest of the area.

Following the War of 1812, the Delaware Indians were driven from their homelands in Ohio, Illinois, and Indiana and relocated in the Ozark Mountains. On arriving, they established settlements near the James River in southwestern Missouri, and by 1820 were operating productive farms. With the passage of more time, the Delaware were eventually joined by the Shawnee, Kickapoo, and Potowatomi. Like the Delaware, these tribes had also been evicted from their homes in the East.

It was sometime during the removal of these tribes to the Ozarks that the Yoachum family arrived. They moved into the James River valley and established a farm. Between growing corn, beans, and squash, trapping and fishing the streams, and hunting wild game in the forests, the Yoachums managed to eke out a comfortable living. The name Yoachum has been found in the literature with a number of different spellings, including Yocum, Yokum, Joachim, Yoakum, Yochum, and Yoachum.

James Yoachum was born in Kentucky in 1772. One year later his brother, Solomon, arrived. Two years later another brother, whose name has been lost to history, came into the world. While the boys were still young, the family moved to Illinois and tried farming. Though James was regarded as a hard and competent worker, he found the daily drudgery of farm labor unsatisfactory. Possessed of wanderlust, he left the family farm, as well as a pregnant wife, and traveled to the Ozark Mountains to seek his fortune as a trapper. He was only eighteen.

During his first year in the Ozarks, James experienced considerable success. He decided to return to Illinois and convince his brothers to join him. On arriving home, however, James discovered that months earlier his wife had died only minutes after giving birth to a son. The boy, named Jacob Levi Yoachum, was taken in by Solomon and his wife.

James remained on the family farm for several years, believing he had an obligation to help out. He despised the tedium of daily toil on the flat Illinois prairie and dreamed often of returning to the Missouri Ozarks. He eventually decided it was time to travel to the distant mountains and trapping. He discussed his plan with his brothers for several nights in a row. By the time James was ready to leave, the brothers had agreed to join him within a year.

After arriving back in the Ozarks, James met and married a young Delaware woman named Winona. They built a small cabin near the confluence of the James and White Rivers and developed a productive farm. It is believed by some that the James River was named for James Yoachum.

As a result of a series of delays, James' brothers were unable to join him until 1815. By the time they arrived, James had most of the river bottom portion of his farm planted in squash and corn and had acquired impressive herds of cattle and horses. His neighbors were Delaware Indians, several of whom had assisted James with the construction of his cabin. The Indians often brought gifts of venison and turkey to the cabin. In turn, James shared a portion of his harvest with the tribe. He gifted several of them with fine horses.

The Yoachums noticed that the Delaware Indians often wore hand-crafted jewelry and ornaments made from high-quality silver, including arm bands, beaded necklaces, and hair fixtures. One day while working in the field with a neighbor, James asked about the source of the silver. The Delaware explained that, many years earlier, an aged Choctaw who lived with the tribe told them of a cave far away in the forest that contained a treasure in silver bars. He explained that the ingots were stacked in a deep chamber shoulder high to a big man. Not far from the cave, explained the Indian, were a number of mines from which the silver had been dug.

James asked the Indian if he would show him the mine. The Delaware explained that a pact had been made between the Choctaw and the Delaware never to reveal the location of the silver.

Years passed, and the valley and its associated farms grew productive and prosperous. So prosperous, in fact, that several covetous and influential politicians and entrepreneurs desired the Delaware's farms. As a result, the federal government was petitioned and soon an Indian-removal process was undertaken. All of the Delaware, Shawnee, Kickapoo, and Potowatomi were kicked off their holdings and moved to Indian Territory to the west, later called Oklahoma.

As his Delaware friends were packing their belongings into wagons and loading them onto horses, the Yoachum brothers arrived to help. They brought gifts for their friends including extra horses, blankets, cooking utensils, and clothes. In gratitude, the Indians agreed to reveal the location of the silver cache and mines to the brothers.

Two weeks after the last of the Delawares had left for Indian Territory, the Yoachums found the cave and the mines. The three brothers agreed never to reveal the location. With one exception, they carried the secret to their graves.

When the brothers decided to retrieve some of the silver, they rode to the site from their farms, loaded several ingots on horseback, and returned. The trip took three days. In time, they accumulated a sizeable stack of ingots. They claimed that hundreds remained in the cave.

More time passed, and more settlers arrived in the region of the James River valley. In response to the growing demand for goods, trading posts were established, and the Yoachum brothers grew more involved with the commerce of the day. One of the largest trading posts in the region was the James Fork Trading Post which was managed by a man named William Gilliss. The Yoachum brothers were regular customers at the post. Even though they had the largest and most productive farms in the area, and though they supplemented their harvest with the hunting of game, they often traded pelts at the post for staples such as salt, sugar, flour, and coffee.

The trading post was owned by a business firm called Menard and Valle. The company headquarters were located in St. Genevieve, Missouri. Colonel Pierre Menard had spent a great deal of time and energy creating good relationships with the Indian tribes and settlers in the area, and he watched the business operations of the James Fork Trading Post closely.

Among the newcomers to the region were small companies of French trappers. The trappers aligned themselves with Menard and he, in turn, grew protective of their interests. Since the Yoachums were considered outsiders by Menard, he instructed Gilliss that they and other non-Frenchmen in the region purchase their supplies with cash. He insisted that, save for the Frenchmen, the medium of exchange would no longer be furs or even raw gold and silver, but federally issued coin and currency. The Yoachums, though rich in silver, had no money.

James decided Menard would not get the best of him. Using some simple blacksmith tools, the brothers made some dies, melted down some of the accumulated silver, rolled it out into sheets, and stamped out their own coins. The Yoachum-produced coins were slightly larger than those issued by the federal government. On one side was stamped "United States of America" and "1 dollar." The other side bore the inscriptions "Yoachum" and "1822."

During the few months following the production of the first batch of coins, thousands of them found their way into circulation, all placed there by the Yoachums. Soon, most residents of this part of the Ozarks were spending the coins for all kinds of purchases. As manager of the trading post, Gilliss eagerly accepted them. When the first of the coins began arriving at his post, he examined them closely and judged them to be made of the purest silver. In time, the Yoachum Dollars were more common in this part of the Ozarks than government-issued money.

This renegade economic system worked well for many years, and all of the residents were happy with the way things were going. Few people outside of this remote part of the Ozark Mountain had ever heard of the Yoachum dollars.

It was too good to last. In 1845, the government sent a surveying crew into the Ozarks to determine section lines and county boundaries as new lands were being opened up for purchase. As a result, settlers in the area were notified that they would be required to abide by specific homestead laws relative to securing titles to the property on which they lived. Part of that requirement was to pay a filing fee at the government office in Springfield.

Dozens of James River residents, along with several others who wished to purchase some of the new lands made available, arrived at the Springfield office. When they tried to pay their fees with Yoachum dollars they were refused. The government agent in charge explained to them that, according to an 1833 federal regulation, it was illegal to deal in anything but federally issued coin. He told the settlers that unless they paid their fees with legitimate United States money they would not be permitted to have titles to their land.

The settlers, already exhausted from the long journey to Springfield, grew enraged at what they regarded as an arbitrary decision. Several of them pointed rifles and pistols at the agent and told him that the Yoachum dollars meant more to the residents of the Ozarks than government money and it had been that way for years. They instructed him to accept their payment in the dollars or be killed. Fearing for his life, the agent accepted the Yoachum dollars and granted each applicant a valid certificate to his land.

The agent, a dedicated government employee, shipped the Yoachum dollars to authorities in Washington D.C. along with an explanation of what had occurred. When the coins were unpacked at the nation's capitol, they were examined and found to be composed of almost pure silver. In fact, they contained more silver than the government-issued dollars.

While some wanted to levy charges of counterfeiting against the Yoachums, they were dissuaded when federal authorities explained there was no clear attempt to duplicate U.S. government-minted coins. They were, however, concerned about the proliferation of non-federal money circulating throughout the region. After a series of discussions, the government wired the Springfield office and ordered the agent to confiscate the Yoachum dollars and determine the location of their silver mine.

Weeks passed, and the agent arrived at the home of James Yoachum. He announced to James that he had come to examine the silver mine. James, pointing a shotgun at the agent, ordered him away. The agent fled, but one week later he returned with a contingent of eight heavily armed and menacing looking federal troopers. When James responded to the knock at his door, the agent explained the official position of the United States government relative to locally cast silver dollars. He told Yoachum that he was officially being discouraged from manufacturing and distributing any more of the dollars in the future.

James Yoachum was never anything but law-abiding and patriotic. He explained he never willfully intended to do anything illegal, and that he continued manufacturing the dollars in response to the economic needs of his neighbors. He told the agent he would cease manufacturing the dollars but he refused to reveal the existence of the mine, claiming it was none of the government's business. Following hours of discussions, the government agent acceded. He agreed not to prosecute if the Yoachums ceased production of the dollars. The location of the old Spanish mines as well as the treasure cave remained a secret.

More years passed and in 1848 James Yoachum died. One story maintains that he was felled with a severe fever for days and died in his sleep. Another story claims he and his wife, Winona, were killed in a cave-in at one of the mines while retrieving some silver.

After burying James, the surviving brothers decided to travel to California. They had heard stories about the gold that could be found in that state and the notion of prospecting for it appealed to their sense of adventure. Before leaving, according to the legend, the brothers gave the dies used in casting the silver dollars to one of the family members who owned a grist mill near the James River. A search of historical records reveals that a nephew of James Yoachum did, in fact, own and operate a grist mill not far from James' residence during that time.

The brothers sold their farms, loaded their belongings and families into wagons, and departed for California. They were never seen in the Ozarks again. While it has never been verified, a story circulated around the Missouri Ozarks years later that the two Yoachum families perished while crossing the Rocky Mountains on their way west. One version of the story has them being swept away in a flash flood; another has them killed by Indians. With their deaths went the knowledge of the secret location of the silver mines and treasure cave.

Year later, James' son, Jacob Levi, told his own son that after the visit by the government agent the three brothers went to the site and sealed off the mines and the cave so no one could ever find them. Jacob often heard his father describe the location of the site – the valley, the ridges, the forest – but though he searched for years he was never able to find it for himself. He related what he knew about the location to his son, Tom. Tom, a long time resident of Galena, Missouri, also searched for the silver but with no success.

The legend of the Yoachum silver dollars has been told and retold many times for nearly two hundred years. As with most such tales, each retelling is likely filled with embellishments. In fact, there are a number of different versions of the legend. One version tells that, in order to find the treasure cave, the Yoachum brothers followed an Indian to it one afternoon. As the Indian was removing silver from the cave, the brothers allegedly killed him.

Another version claims there was no silver mine or treasure cave at all. It was told that, prior to the arrival of the Yoachums in the area of the James River valley, the relocation of the Delaware Indians by the federal government had long been in place. In addition to the lands assigned to members of the tribe, each Indian family was provided with four thousand dollars in silver coins. The Yoachums, greedy for the silver, began making and selling liquor to the Indians, which was against the law. To avoid being caught in possession of the Indian money, the brothers melted it down and cast their own coins using the homemade dies. In order to cover their illegal activities, the brothers made up the story of finding the silver in the old Spanish mines and a treasure cave. According to researcher Lynn Morrow, the brothers were reluctant to reveal the location of the mines and cave for the simple reason that they never existed.

The above version suggests that the Yoachum brothers leaned toward outlawry. Documents in the possession of the Missouri Historical Society Archives support such a notion. They reveal that a man named John Campbell was named the Indian agent for the James River valley region around 1820. Part of Campbell's job was to be on the lookout for unscrupulous white settlers who wanted to take advantage of the Delaware Indians. By 1822, Campbell had compiled a list of such men. It includes the name Solomon Yoachum and notes that he may have been involved in selling liquor to the Indians. It also revealed that Solomon,

James, and the third brother were evicted from the region for not paying a filing fee on the land.

Yet another version of the legend has the Yoachum brothers leaving the James River area and settling a short distance away and near the mouth of the Finley River. Here, it was said, they operated whiskey and brandy stills. It was claimed that the Yoachum made the finest peach brandy in the country.

Researcher Morrow claims the Yoachums were aware that their silver dollar scheme would be short-lived. When the Delaware Indians were relocated in Indian Territory as a result of the James Fort Treaty of 1829, the source of their silver for manufacturing coins dried up. Immediately after the removal, the Yoachum dollars became scarce.

Regardless of which version of the tale one accepts, the fact remains that the Yoachum dollars did exist and thousands of them were made.

A long time Missouri Ozarks resident named Homer Johnson contributed some insight into the Yoachum dollar legend. Johnson lived all of his life near Breadtray Mountain. His grandfather, Jefferson Johnson, was the boyhood friend of Robert Yoachum, the son of Jacob Levi Yoachum, and the two often played together as children. One afternoon, the boys decided to go riding. As they were saddling two horses in the Yoachum barn, Jefferson Johnson saw a barrel that was filled almost to the top with Yoachum dollars. He estimated there were several thousand coins in the barrel. He had not seen any before or since.

A number of the Yoachum silver dollars are in the possession of collectors. A man from St. Louis whose identity has never been verified, reported that while he was metal detecting near Branson in 1974, he discovered a cache of 236 Yoachum dollars. It is estimated that thousands of them remain to be found.

Treasure hunters and collectors have long wondered what became of the barrel of Yoachum silver dollars Jefferson Johnson saw as a child. They have also long wondered what happened to the dies used to make the coins. The dies were presumed lost or discarded until a remarkable discovery was made in 1983. On March 11 of that year, J.R. Blunk of Galena was digging near a riverbank not far from some property that was once part of the original Yoachum settlement by the James River. Blunk unearthed a mass of wax. When he broke open the large ball of wax, he found two short sections of iron rod. After scraping the wax from one end of the rod, he noticed the reverse lettering of the name "Yoachum." On the other rod he was able to discern, "1 Dollar."

As a result of the interest generated by his discovery, Blunk spent the next few months researching the legend of the Yoachum silver dollars. In the process, he found the names of several collectors who owned samples of the original coins. He contacted one of the collectors, obtained one of the coins, and found that it matched perfectly with the dies he found. To make certain, Blunk brought the dies and coin to a professional numismatist named Fred Wineberg. After a thorough examination, Wineberg concluded Blunk had found the original dies for the Yoachum silver dollars.

Still missing, however, are thousands of Yoachum dollars. What became of the barrel filled with the coins seen in the old Yoachum barn by Jefferson Johnson? How many of the Yoachum dollars were hidden, lost, or otherwise disposed of when the federal government banned their circulation?

It is quite possible that a fortune in Yoachum silver dollars is still packed away in some dusty Ozark attic or barn. In 1992, an antique car collector traveled to a farm located in the James River valley. An old couple was trying to sell a 1950s era Buick that had been parked in their barn for thirty years. The collector drove from Little Rock, Arkansas, and spent an afternoon with the sellers as he examined the old car. He made an offer, they accepted, and he made arrangements to have it picked up and delivered to his home.

While he was chatting with the husband, the collector wandered around the barn in search of other antiques. He found some hubcaps for a 1952 Studebaker and a hood ornament he couldn't identify. As he examined the contents of an old wooden milk box, he found twelve odd coins. Dusting them off, he noted each one was inscribed with the name "Yoachum." When he asked the old farmer about them, he was told they were "worthless counterfeits, no good to nobody." The farmer said he could have them. He told the collector that a number of folks around this part of the Ozark Mountains still possessed some of the Yoachum dollars. He also said that he knew a man who lived in the next county who had a "barrel full of them."

Weeks after returning to his home in Little Rock, the car collector undertook some research and learned the story behind the Yoachum dollars. He also learned that a barrel full of the coins, such as was described by the old man who sold him the Buick, would be worth an incredible fortune. He decided he would return to the mountains to speak with the fellow, learn the identity of the owner of the barrel full of coins, and try to obtain it.

On arriving at the small farm, the collector learned that the old man had died. His wife had often heard the story of someone who possessed thousands of the Yoachum silver dollars stored in an old barrel in his barn, but she did not know his identity.

Since 1992, the collector has been traveling to the James River area in search of the missing Yoachum dollars. In addition to the lost coins, the silver mines which originally yielded the ore have never been located.

I got repeatedly led (randomization) to watch "The Strong box" Seinfeld ep lately, including today (8/29/2014) after & earlier at supper, God led me (random.) to read cemetary gold. In the ep, they dig in a cemetary (pet)

F E V: 13
5 5 3?

Look up church hollow
on maps on GT sites, etc.
Appr. distance from F.S.

Check springfield
for dealers who
have a Whites TM 808.
Also, CL - Springfbd.

Cemetery Gold

The tiny community of Church Hollow in the Missouri
Ozarks is but a memory to only a few people living today.
The wood-frame church served the religious and social
needs of the few settlers who arrived in the region during
the late 1800s. Next to the church was a small cemetery,
the headstones made from local limestone and the
inscriptions carved by hand. Somewhere in this century-
and-a-half-old cemetery an iron kettle was buried during
the Civil War. It was filled to the top with gold coins.

Church Hollow was one of several small communities
located in Cedar County, a three-day wagon ride over
rough and rugged terrain located northwest of Springfield.
Cedar County contributed a handful of fighting men to the
Union army. Only one returned.

The survivor was a veteran of the bloody battle of
Wilson's Creek. The violence and atrocities he witnessed
there caused him to lose his mind. He became so crazed
and disoriented that he was given a discharge and allowed
to return to his home.

The ex-soldier was taken in by family members but
never regained his sanity. He remained a shattered and

55

confused man until his death. The veteran spoke continuously yet incoherently about a pot of gold he claimed was buried in the cemetery next to the church. At first, the story generated some interest among a few of the citizens, but they soon believed that it was merely the ravings of a deranged mind. As time passed, few people paid any attention to him at all.

As he grew older, the ex-soldier was able to hold down a job. Though he continued to suffer nightmares as a result of his war experiences, they grew less severe with time. He married and had children. Though he occasionally became lost in the memories of those violent days, he managed to provide for his family.

With the passage of years, his memory returned, slowly at first. With each passing week, he was able to recall events from his past that had previously eluded him. One oft-repeated memory was one involving his two best friends. He remembered that as young men in their early twenties they received information about the ongoing War Between the States. They all decided to join the army. They pooled their savings, inheritances, and proceeds from the recent sales of a farm, placed them in an old iron kettle, and buried it somewhere safe until the war was over and they could return home. During this time there were no banks nearer than Springfield, and it was a common practice for families to bury their money.

The iron kettle was filled nearly to the top with twenty dollar gold pieces. With great difficulty, the three men dragged the heavy kettle to the graveyard next to the Church Hollow church and buried it. A short distance from the cemetery they found a large flat stone. On the surface they scratched directions to the cache, along with the

Stone is gone

amount of gold they had placed in the kettle. They covered the stone with dirt and forest debris so no one would see it.

For years the ex-soldier waited for his two friends to return home so they could dig up the kettle filled with gold coins, but they never did. In time, he learned that they had both been killed. He decided to travel to the graveyard and retrieve the treasure himself.

When he arrived at the Church Hollow cemetery, he became disoriented. He could not remember the exact location where the kettle was buried. Then he remembered the flat rock on which the location had been marked. He searched for days but was never able to find it. He noticed that the place where the rock was hidden had been cleared and cleaned. When he inquired, he was told that a few years earlier some citizens wanted to expand the graveyard and set about clearing off that particular space. All of the rocks had been removed, but no one remembered where they were taken.

For the rest of his life, the ex-soldier visited the graveyard every week. He walked around the enclosure hoping he might find something that would key his memory to where the fortune in gold coins was buried. He died without ever finding it.

Church Hollow is a ghost town today. The old church is no longer standing and weeds and briars have encroached upon and taken over the cemetery. Here and there one can find remains of the fence that once surrounded it. Somewhere inside the small graveyard lying just a few inches below the surface is an iron kettle filled with gold coins, a lost treasure that would be worth an impressive fortune if found.

The Lost Treasure of Alonzus Hall

During the Civil War and for many years following, the Ozark Mountains were home to a number of outlaws who preyed on settlers, Indians, travelers, trappers, and prospectors. During that time, the Ozarks offered little in the way of law enforcement and protection, and what could be found was inefficient and scattered.

Into this environment rode Alonzus Hall. Hall was described as a handsome young man with blue eyes, a keen wit, and a disarming smile. Hall made friends easily and was popular with the ladies in every settlement he visited. He was also a robber and murderer. The violent-prone Hall led a band of hardened criminals throughout the Ozarks, taking what they wanted and leaving a trail of blood behind. Hall possessed a bottomless spirit of adventure that he tried to satisfy at all costs. Fearless, he reveled in danger, and always sought more daring holdups and raids. This eventually led to his undoing.

Hall and his gang ranged in the Ozark Mountains from just north of Springfield and south to Arkansas. Rarely did he encounter resistance to his ravages. Because law enforcement was either nonexistent or inefficient, he was seldom pursued. He pillaged with impunity, spreading terror throughout the hills and valleys of the range.

In April, 1862, Hall and his band of six killers rode into the settlement of Centralia. Wielding guns and knives, they robbed the bank of $52,000 in gold coins. After shooting up the town, they rode south, knowing they were safe from pursuit. During their flight, they paused long enough to rob two farmsteads. After asking for and receiving food for themselves and some grain for their horses, Hall and his cutthroats forced the generous farmers to hand over all of their money. Following this, they rode deep into the safety of the Ozarks. Or so they thought.

Camped alongside the Frisco railroad tracks twenty-five miles west of Springfield was a company of Union soldiers under the command of Captain W.F. McCullough. Along with his military obligations, McCullough kept track of Hall's depredations. If the opportunity ever presented itself, McCullough was determined to go after the outlaw and bring him to justice. One day after the bank robbery, McCullough received orders to pursue Hall and his gang and bring them in at any cost.

McCullough learned that the Hall gang traveled southward after the bank robbery. They had been following the old Wilderness Road and were last seen in Greene County. Intent on overtaking the outlaws, McCullough ordered the soldiers to ride for twelve hours without stopping save to water and rest their horses. The trail passed through Greene County, Christian County, and then into Stone County. After the company of soldiers entered this rugged environment of the Ozark Mountains filled with narrow hollows and wooded ridges, the captain sent out scouts to interview homesteaders to try and learn Hall's whereabouts.

On the evening of the second day of pursuit, one of the scouts reported to McCullough that he had learned the outlaws were camped under a limestone ledge near the bank of the White River about one mile away. At the time the scout found the outlaws, one of Hall's lookouts also spotted him. An hour later when the scout saw the approaching soldiers, he raced back to the campsite to alert his companions.

Hall and the bandits had been in the process of splitting up the money they had taken from the bank and the farmers. On hearing the news of the approaching soldiers, they placed each share in a buckskin bag, a total of $62,000. Hall and two companions carried the bags to a nearby cave. There, they scooped out a shallow trench into which they placed the bags and then refilled the hole. Atop this they piled rocks to conceal any traces of digging.

As he laid the last rock atop the cache site, Hall heard gunfire coming from the campsite. The soldiers had arrived and engaged the remaining outlaws in battle. Hall and his two accomplices raced back to the camp to join the fight.

McCullough had launched a vicious attack on Hall's gang. Clearly outnumbered and outgunned, the gang had no chance against the company of troopers. The fight lasted less than five minutes. Hall's six henchmen lay dead and Hall was dying from a stomach wound.

Hall was bandaged, placed in a wagon bed, and transported to a temporary bivouac area next to the White River near present-day Reeds Spring. He was sedated and his wound cleaned out, but there was little that could be done. The following morning he was taken to the military hospital at Springfield. The attending surgeon, Dr.

Boucher, found that the bullet had done irreparable damage to Hall's lower intestines. Boucher informed authorities that the outlaw would not live more than one or two days.

Several hours later, Hall regained consciousness. After Hall cried out in pain for several minutes, Dr. Boucher arrived at his bedside and informed him of his condition and his fate. Hall grew silent, then angry. An hour later, after cursing and crying, he became resigned to the fact that he was going to die.

The following morning, Hall asked for Dr. Boucher. When the surgeon arrived, he found Hall in relatively good spirits. Hall asked Boucher if he could dictate a confession to him. The doctor agreed to take Hall's statement. After securing a hospital journal, he sat by the outlaw's bedside and took copious notes as Hall related the events associated with the recent robberies.

Hall described in detail all that had occurred from the time of the bank holdup to the arrival of the soldiers at their White River campsite. He said that a total of $62,000 was buried in a shallow cave near the old ferryboat landing where the Wilderness Road met the White River. He asked Boucher to do what he could to retrieve the money and return it to the farmers and the bank.

Boucher took several pages of notes in the journal. After a few minutes, Hall grew exhausted and was unable to continue. Boucher checked the dressing on his wound, injected him with a pain killer, and left. The next morning when the surgeon arrived to check on the outlaw, Alonzus Hall was dead.

Dr. Boucher was uncertain about what to do with the information on the buried cache. His military training told him he should inform his superiors immediately, but the temptation of coming into possession of a great fortune tugged at him. With a dream of becoming richer, Boucher hid the journal and told no one of Hall's deathbed confession. Boucher went about his duties as post surgeon and awaited the day when he would be able to travel to the place where the Wilderness Road met the White River, locate the small cave, and retrieve the gold and money.

It was not to be. Within a few weeks, Dr. Boucher was transferred to a large military post in the East. As he packed for the move, he hid the journal in a cabinet filled with hospital files.

Dr. Boucher was never able to return to southwestern Missouri to retrieve the buried cache. His commitment to the military lasted several more years. By the time he was mustered out, he suffered from health problems that kept him from traveling. More years passed, and employees at the Springfield hospital found the old journal while cleaning out dated paperwork from some file cabinets.

By 1900, several people had seen the notes written by Dr. Boucher. The descriptions of the robberies and the burying of the gold and money were quite detailed and vivid. In the journal, it was written that the cache was located in a small cave not far from the outlaws' campsite under the overhanging limestone ledge. The cave was described as slightly illuminated as a result of the sun shining through an opening in the roof. The gold and money were buried in the center of the shaft of light.

The point where the old Wilderness Road meets the White River ferry crossing is easy to locate. It is noted on several maps of the region. It would therefore seem a simple task to locate the small cave where the outlaw loot was buried. The principal difficulty with finding the cache has to do with the fact that the area has been submerged as a result of the backed up waters of Table Rock Lake.

Not far from the presumed cache is the Kimberling Bridge. Some have opined that the construction the bridge may have obliterated any traces of the cave. Others maintain that the location of the bridge would suggest that the cache site was not impacted at all and that the treasure still lies under several feet of lake water.

Lost Copper Mine on Jack's Fork Creek

Over the years, a number of so-called experts have claimed that gold and silver cannot be found in the limestone rock that makes up most of the Ozark Mountains. The number of productive gold and silver mines that have been operated in the Ozarks from the sixteenth century to the present demonstrates that the experts are not always correct. It is true that limestone, as with most sedimentary rock, is not a common source of precious metals. What the experts neglect to mention, or even notice, however, is that the Ozark Mountains are underlain by granitic rock, its origin associated with below-ground volcanic activity. It is in such rock that gold, silver, and other metals are often formed. And throughout the Ozarks, granite outcrops are not rare.

Gold and silver are not the only metals that have been discovered in this mountain range. During the 1850s, a man named John Slater discovered a rich copper deposit. During the time he worked the mine, he had earned over $50,000 for his effort, a handsome sum in those days.

Slater entered the Ozarks in search of gold and silver. He prospected likely outcrops in the region of the Current River some four miles above the mouth of Jack's Fork Creek. For weeks he lived in the area, moving from camp to camp in search of ore, but had no luck. Then, Slater accidentally discovered a rich deposit of copper.

At the first opportunity, Slater traveled to the nearest settlement to file a claim. Before doing so, he examined records and discovered that someone owned the land on which the copper deposit was located. Not wishing to relinquish his find, Slater filed on an adjacent parcel of land and mined the copper in secret.

Slater built a crude shack on his land. He traveled to town from time to time to purchase coffee, flour, and other staples. Because the woods were rich with wild game such as deer, turkey, and squirrels, he never lacked for meat. For four years he lived thus as he dug the copper from the ground. After subjecting it to a crude refining process, he rafted it down the river where it was eventually sold in New Orleans.

During the time Slater was working in his secret mine, the federal government sent surveyors into the Ozark Mountains. Boundaries were established, homestead claims were verified or denied, and the land and its inhabitants were inventoried. The survey revealed that an error was made when Slater filed on his land. Legally, it belonged to someone else. Slater appealed, but the U.S. government had the final word. Slater was informed he had to vacate the parcel of land.

Slater was inclined to hire a lawyer and contest the decision in court, but feared that any attention given his case might lead to the discovery of the copper deposit. Slater decided to shut down the mine and abandon the area for a time. He took great pains to cover the entrance to the mine so that no one else would ever find it.

A short time later, Slater moved to St. Louis where he found work. He intended to save his money and in a few years return to the Jack's Fork Creek area and attempt to purchase the land on which the copper mine was located.

After two years in St. Louis, Slater became ill. He died before he had the opportunity to carry out his plan. When the story of his secret copper mine was revealed, prospectors arrived in the Jack's Fork Creek area to search for it. While small deposits of the metal were located at a variety of locations, Slater's copper mine has never been found.

The Lost Gold of Preacher Keith

One of the most commonly related tales of lost treasure in Missouri is the one about the strange preacher who hid a fortune in gold coins. W.M. Keith was an itinerant preacher who arrived in the Missouri Ozarks from the Red River Valley of Oklahoma near where that muddy stream and the Chisholm Trail intersect. His descendants, who still live in the Missouri Ozarks, claim he left Oklahoma and traveled east with only the clothes on his back and carrying a well-used Bible. Others suggest he was forced to leave the area but offered no explanation why.

A short time after arriving in the area of Reeds Spring, Missouri, Keith built a small one-room log cabin near a creek. Keith was a tall, thin man and in later years was said to resemble Abraham Lincoln. He was gangly and uncoordinated and walked in a strange manner. Keith also had a habit of talking to himself as he traveled the roads and trails of the Ozark Mountains. It was said he walked from dawn until dusk with no apparent destination. Settlers would occasionally find Keith sleeping in their barn. When discovered, he would launch into a sermon and quote from the pages of the Bible. Invariably, he would be invited to dinner.

In addition to relying on his neighbors for an occasional meal, Keith was described as a skilled hunter and lived well off the land. In addition, he trapped animals and sold the pelts and took seasonal jobs with area farmers. Though most residents of the valley in which he lived considered him odd, he was regarded as a good worker and was generally well-liked.

After living in the area of Reeds Spring for a year, Keith decided to devote most of his time to preaching. On Sundays he visited outlying areas and conducted church services for any and all who would come to listen to him. He had a booming voice, and it was said that when he began his services in a barn or under a tree, his message could be heard a half-mile away, luring even more to his make-shift chapel.

In time, Keith met and married a young girl. He moved his bride, Lee, into the tiny cabin. Within a year, she bore a child, the first of many. Between what he collected from preaching and selling furs, Keith grew corn which he sold to neighbors. The hillside near his cabin was cleared and planted, and each year he grew a healthy crop. In addition, Keith planted an orchard. In time, his peach, apple, and cherry trees were producing fruit. Keith took great pride in his orchard, and spent many hours pruning the trees and seeing that they received water.

In 1850, Keith learned about the discovery of gold in California and the successes miners and prospectors were experiencing. The lure of finding his fortune in what he considered a faraway land thrilled Keith and he was unable to resist the call. Bidding his wife and children goodbye, he set out for the Golden State with the hope of striking it rich.

Keith experienced great successes in the California gold fields. After two years of working twelve to fourteen hours a day panning gold from the streams in the Sierra Nevada Mountains, he had accumulated what would be regarded as a fortune. He converted his ore into gold coins. This done, he booked passage on a ship, packed his gold in a wooden trunk, sailed from San Francisco around the southern tip of South America and thence up to New Orleans. There, he purchased two mules and a number of leather sacks into which he placed his gold coins. Leading the mules, Keith walked the entire distance back to his home in the Ozarks.

News of the preacher's return, along with his impressive wealth, soon spread throughout the region. Keith grew visibly annoyed that so many of his neighbors became aware of his fortune. He found himself fielding requests for loans, all of which he denied. As time passed, he grew suspicious of his neighbors, and became convinced that they were all intent on stealing his gold. When visitors arrived at his cabin, he chased them away at the point of a shotgun. He did not sleep nights, preferring to stay awake to guard his gold.

The paranoia and lack of sleep was taking a toll on Preacher Keith. He decided to hide his gold in a place where no one would ever think to search. He loaded his coins once again onto the mules and carried them some distance from his cabin into the woods. When he was certain he was not being observed, he cached his gold coins in a secret location, one that has generated a mystery that remains to this day.

For unexplained reasons, Keith never revealed to his family where he hid the gold. Descendants who have been interviewed claimed that when Keith left the cabin to hide his gold, he was gone for no longer than an hour. Some believe that the coins were hidden in one of the many caves that can be found in the region.

A few who have researched the legend of the eccentric Preacher Keith and his lost treasure are convinced the gold is buried in or near his orchard. They point out that Keith talked about his orchard more than he did his family, and that it held a level of great pride for him. It was said that at the times Keith needed cash for some purchase, he would leave the cabin and walk in the direction of the orchard. Moments later he would return with a twenty-dollar gold piece. On the few occasions he was asked about his fortune, he stated that the gold grew on the trees in his orchard.

Another version related to the caching of his gold coins has to do with the belief that he walled up the entrance to one of the caves in a nearby mountain and hid his gold within. This belief comes from the fact that Keith was sometimes seen hauling slabs of rock into the woods some distance from his cabin. He would be gone for several hours. If anyone came near, he would chase them away, threatening to shoot them with his shotgun. When he returned home at the end of the day, his overalls and boots would be coated in mortar. When asked by family members, he referred to a "room" he was building in which he was going to hide his gold so that no one would ever find it.

One evening, he returned to the cabin with a bleeding thumb. He explained that he had accidentally struck it with a hammer while fashioning a door. He stated that he had spent the day making a wooden door that would fit the opening for the room he was building. He said that the door was made from heavy oak timbers that he cut and planed himself and that it was eight feet tall and four feet wide. He also claimed that door was fastened shut with a stout lock.

Though no one is certain of the source, a rumor circulated throughout that part of the Ozarks that Preacher Keith had built a casket and placed it in the small room of the walled-up cave. It was said that Keith told his family that he constructed a casket of pine boards. He explained that when he was ready to die, he planned on locking himself up in the secret room and lying down in his casket. The casket, the rumor continued, was surrounded by Preacher Keith's gold coins.

It was said that Preacher Keith visited his private hoard at least once each week for years. During this time his family had no inkling of where he went. Once in a while, one of his children attempted to follow him, but the preacher remained elusive. Countless times they asked him where his gold was hidden, but he only laughed and said that no one would ever find it.

As Preacher Keith grew older, his behavior became more erratic and unpredictable. Many of the area residents believed he had gone insane, and fewer people showed up for his Sunday sermons.

None of this appeared to bother Keith. He continued to hunt and trap and sell his pelts in town. He continued to grow corn on the hillside and harvest fruit from his orchard. He continued to provide for his family, though he spent little of his gold.

One morning after finishing his breakfast, Preacher Keith told his family he was going hunting. He picked up his rifle, wiped it off with his shirt-tail, and left the cabin. Members of his family watched him as he walked out into the woods. He was never seen again.

Many who are close to the story of Preacher Keith assume he went to his secret room in some cave, locked himself in, and laid down in his casket to die in the company of his twenty-dollar gold pieces. When Keith was reported missing the following day, neighbors combed the hills and valleys in search of him. They found neither the man nor the cave. After a week, the search was halted.

Two months following the disappearance of Preacher Keith, a man was deep in the woods hunting for game when he came upon a badly decomposed body. It was found in an abandoned orchard in a hollow four miles south of Reeds Spring. The hunter described the remains as seated on the ground and leaning against the trunk of a cherry tree with a rifle lying across its lap. Nearby, a shovel lay on the ground.

The hunter went for help. Later in the day he and three companions returned to the site and examined the remains. They found no wounds or anything else to help determine the manner of death. They concluded that whoever it was must have died from a heart attack. They buried the man beneath the tree where he was found.

When they finished their chore, the four men left the gravesite and walked through the orchard. They noticed that several holes had been recently dug as if someone was looking for something.

When word of the dead man reached the Keith family several days later, they paid a visit to the hunter who had made the discovery. He described the clothing and boots worn by the deceased and produced the rifle he had found on the man. The family concluded the dead man was Preacher Keith.

Many believe that the abandoned orchard in which the body of Preacher Keith had been found held the secret to his hidden gold. They are convinced that his cryptic comments about the gold growing on trees referred not to the orchard near his cabin but the one in which his body was discovered. The holes in the orchard were puzzling. Had Preacher Keith dug up his treasure and hid it somewhere else? Or had he forgotten where it was buried and dug the holes in search of it? Did the effort of digging the holes bring on a heart attack which ultimately killed him?

Had Preacher Keith dug up the gold coins he possibly had hidden in the old orchard and carried them to his secret cave? Did he return to the orchard for more when he suffered a heart attack? And what of the rumors of the empty casket lying somewhere in a secret cave not far from Preacher Keith's cabin? To date, no one has ever found the mysterious cave or the fortune in gold coins.

Silver Coin Cache

Before the Ozark Mountains of Missouri saw the arrival of settlers, farmers, and ranchers during and after the Civil War, it was a preferred location for trappers. Populations of beaver and other fur-bearing mammals were large and healthy, and during that time good money could be made supplying hatters and others in the east with pelts.

As in the Rocky Mountains, the trapping of beaver in the Ozarks was not without its hazards. Hostile Indian tribes populated the Ozarks, and because of the general absence of law enforcement, the region became a haven for outlaws on the run. If one was willing to take the risks apparent in the Ozarks, one could earn a good living.

By the late 1800s, most of the beaver had been trapped out of the Ozark Mountains. Along with the depleted resource, the demand for furs lessened. As a result, only a few determined trappers remained in the region pursuing their trade, and most sought other ways to make a living during the course of a year. One such trapper was a Frenchman named Boucher. Boucher built a log cabin near today's town of West Plains where he lived with his wife and daughter.

In spite of the setbacks that affected the trapping industry, Boucher remained optimistic. In December of 1901, he purchased additional traps and went about the business of setting them out in the hope that this would be a good year and that the harvest would be bountiful. It was turning into an unseasonably cold winter and Boucher knew this would cause the pelts to grow thick and full. Come spring, Boucher believed his harvest would bring good prices in the market.

Following the last frost of spring, Boucher loaded his pelts onto several mules, bade his family goodbye, and traveled to the trading post at Cape Girardeau on the Mississippi River, some 150 miles to the northeast. Though the market for furs had slackened, his pelts sold for top dollar. Using some of the money, he purchased supplies and undertook the long journey back to West Plains. In his saddlebags he carried 400 silver dollars.

Late on the afternoon of the second day of travel, Boucher noticed that he was being followed by two men on horseback. He remembered seeing them in Cape Girardeau and suspected that they knew about the money in his saddlebags. He reasoned that the men would wait until he stopped to make camp for the night and then attempt to rob him. Boucher decided that instead of setting up camp, he would keep riding in hope of reaching home earlier than planned. He paused only long enough to rest his horses and allow them to water and graze. Not wishing to take the time to build a fire, he subsisted only on the jerky and hardtack he carried in his saddlebags.

Just after dawn of the fourth day of traveling, Boucher was only three miles from his cabin. He turned in the saddle and saw the two men behind him approaching at a gallop and clearly intent on catching up with him. Boucher spurred his horse, and with his pack animals in tow raced toward home.

As Boucher rode up to the front door of his cabin, he called to his wife and she came out onto the porch. He told her he was being followed and that she should send the pursuers down the road toward Springfield. He told her he was going to ride over to a nearby pond, bury his silver coins, and return when the pursuers had departed. Leading his pack animals, Boucher rode away into the woods toward a pond a quarter of a mile away.

Within minutes, the two riders approached the cabin and called out. Mrs. Boucher came out onto the porch, her young daughter in tow and clutching at her dress. The men asked her if she had seen anyone pass by during the past few minutes. She pointed toward the road that led to Springfield and said a man had gone that way. Just as they were about to ride away, one of the riders spotted the tracks of Boucher's horse and pack animals. The men turned their horses and followed them down the trail that led into the woods.

For the rest of the day and throughout the night, Mrs. Boucher awaited the return of her husband. When he had not arrived at dawn, she walked into the town of West Plains to seek help. After hearing her story, a town constable organized a search party and returned to the Boucher cabin. The search centered near the pond, but other than Boucher's horse and one pack animal nothing was found. Boucher was never seen again.

After the search party returned to town, Mrs. Boucher returned to the pond to look for herself. In addition to looking for her husband, she searched for signs of recent digging in hopes of locating the place where the trapper buried his coins. She was unsuccessful.

To this day, no one knows what became of trapper Boucher. Many believe he was killed by his pursuers, but it is unknown whether or not he was able to hide his money before it happened. Since Mrs. Boucher never saw any signs of digging, many were convinced that Boucher threw his coin-filled saddlebags into the pond and road away, only to be killed some distance farther into the woods.

There are those who believe that if the site of the old Boucher cabin could be identified, the nearby pond might be located. They are convinced that a thorough search of the bottom of the pond would yield the 400 silver coins, a treasure that would be worth a great deal of money today. It could also yield the remains of trapper Boucher.

A Fortune in Silver

One of the most compelling tales of lost treasure told around the Ozark Mountains is one involving two men who set out on an adventure and found what many believe to be one of the richest silver mines ever to exist in North America. The discovery also led to their death, and the location of the mine remains a mystery today.

The two men who are at the center of this tale met in St. Louis in 1800. They were both of French descent and both working on the loading docks on the banks of the Mississippi River. For twelve hours a day, they carried goods from the many boats that tied up at the port and stacked them in nearby warehouses.

In a manner never discerned by those who have attempted to research this story, the two friends came into the possession of a treasure map. The map, replete with notations in Spanish, purported to show the location of a rich silver mine in the Ozark Mountains several days travel to the southwest.

One version of this tale states that the silver deposit was discovered by Spaniards and mined for many years. Another version claims that the mine was originally worked by area Indians who harvested the silver for hundreds of years to fashion jewelry and armbands. The Spaniards, according to this version, took over the mine on arriving in the mountain range. The truth has never been discerned.

Purportedly, one morning as the two friends were walking to their jobs at the loading docks, they came across the body of an Indian. In one of the dead man's coat pockets, they found the map. After work that day, they returned to the room they rented and examined their new possession. The notations were in Spanish. The two men had learned enough of the language while working on the docks to determine the meaning of the map. On discovering that it showed the way to a great fortune in silver, they decided to quit their jobs and go in search of it.

Their excitement and enthusiasm were tempered by reality. Given the low pay they received for their labors on the docks, the two had only a few dollars between them. It was not enough to subsidize an expedition deep into the Ozarks in search of the silver. They had to find another way.

The two Frenchmen approached a local businessman with whom they were acquainted. They showed him the map they had found and explained its meaning. The businessman agreed to fund their expedition in exchange for a share of the profits. During the next few days, the two men purchased a pair of good riding horses, a string of pack mules, supplies, and provisions to last for several weeks. Convinced they were in possession of everything they needed to locate the rich silver mine, they rode out of St. Louis toward the Ozark Mountains.

Little noteworthy occurred during the first two days of their journey. Their excitement at finding the silver mine was tempered only slightly by the tedium of the slow travel, broken only when they stopped to prepare a meal and water and rest the horses and mules. On the morning of third day, the drudgery of the plodding travel was broken when one of the men noticed they were being followed.

After casting glances to the rear from time to time, they discovered that they were being tailed by a small party of Indians who remained several hundred yards back. The two friends left the trail and rode across the brushy rolling plain. Several minutes later when they looked back they saw that the Indians left the trail at the same place and continued to follow them.

The two men decided to spur their mounts to a gallop in an attempt to outdistance the Indians. Their pursuers likewise picked up the pace. Finally, one of the men suggested they find a place to hide and allow the Indians to pass them. After rounding a bend in the trail that curved behind a low hill, they spotted a thick grove of trees about a mile away. They headed for it. Once in the grove, they hid the animals and watched the trail. A short time later, the group of Indians came into sight. They reined in their horses at the location where their quarry left the trail. For several minutes they stared at the grove of trees in which the two were hiding. Following some discussion, the Indians continued on down the trail. The two friends made camp in the grove, and the next morning set out once again for the Ozark Mountains, this time keeping a wary eye out for the Indians.

Over the next few days, the two men spotted the Indians from time to time. On one occasion they were on the trail about a mile ahead of them. On another, they were behind them, clearly following but in no apparent hurry to catch up.

At last, the two Frenchmen, referring to the map, noted the land was changing. Instead of the rolling prairies they had ridden through during the previous days, they encountered the rugged foothills of the Ozarks. The grades became steeper, and the trail wound around huge limestone outcrops. As they rode deeper into the range, they wound their way through narrow canyons and dark gorges and across steep and rough ridges. Because of the dense forest, the ever-twisting trail, and the lack of any horizon save for the enclosing ridges, they could not tell if they were still being followed. Then, they found the silver mine.

It was not a mine at all in the sense that there was a shaft that had been excavated. It was a natural cave, one that had been formed as a result of a huge earthquake fracturing and separating the limestone strata resulting in a tent-shaped opening. In splitting the sedimentary rock, the earthquake also exposed an underlying deposit of granite. Deep in this cave and running through the bed of granite was a seam of silver described as being six-feet high and twelve inches across.

Evidence of previous mining lay all about the cave. Hand-forged metal mining tools of great age were scattered about the floor. Nearby, the two men found a crude smelter where the ore was melted down and poured into ingots. A number of ingot molds lay nearby. In addition, they found several skeletons.

The friends spent two days exploring the cave and inventorying its contents. They were convinced that with weeks of patient work excavating and processing the ore, they would be rich men. In the evening when they made camp each man shared his dreams of what he would do with his fortune once they returned to St. Louis. Every evening following dinner, the Frenchmen would record the day's events in his diary.

During the next two weeks, the two men excavated twenty-two pounds of almost pure silver from the vein. One evening as they were packing some of the ore into sacks, they spotted several Indians observing them from a nearby ridge top.

That night, the two men each confessed to having premonitions of disaster if they remained in the area much longer. They decided they should pack what silver they had accumulated, cover the entrance to the mine, and depart for St. Louis before dawn. It was their intention to wait until the threat of Indian presence was gone or diminished before returning to mine more of the silver.

Two hours before dawn, the men finished securing the packs containing their remaining provisions and the silver ore onto the mules. Because there was only a thin sliver of moon in the sky and scattered clouds obscured most of the stars, they went about their business assured they could not be seen. As quietly as possible, the two broke camp and rode away in the darkness.

While the night likely hid their flight from the Indians, it hampered their escape. They had been on the trail for no more than an hour when they realized they had become lost. When dawn broke, they realized they were not on the road that would take them back to St. Louis. Instead, they found themselves several miles west of the silver mine. As they debated which direction they should ride, they noticed that the Indians were following them again.

The friends decided their chances would be improved if they split up. In haste, they divided the silver. Each man took half of the mules and they rode away in different directions.

Because of the orientation of the canyons and trail, the Frenchman rode westward for nearly two days before finding an opportunity to circle northward. After two more days of rough travel, he encountered a road that he was certain would take him to St. Louis. On the evening of the third day of traveling this road, the Frenchman came upon the body of his friend.

The corpse lay in the middle of the road, twenty-five arrows protruding from the torso. His horse and mules were nowhere to be seen. After examining the body, the Frenchman determined that his friend had not been dead for long. Fearing that the Indians were still close by, he leaped upon his horse and rode away. That evening in camp, he sat by the light of the camp fire and recorded the day's events in his journal.

As he finished writing about finding the body of his friend, the Frenchman was about to close the journal and prepare to climb into his bedroll when he saw that he was surrounded by the Indians. Slowly and deliberately, they closed in on him, lances raised and arrows nocked on bowstrings. Attempting to appear nonchalant, he scribbled some final notes on the open page. As the Indians neared, he closed the journal, placing the map to the silver mine between it pages, and stuffed it into his coat pocket. After tossing a small log onto the fire, he rose and awaited his fate.

One week later, a party of trappers traveling down the road toward St. Louis came upon the body of the Frenchman. As two of the trappers excavated a hole in which to bury the dead man, another went through his pockets in search of identification. In this manner, they came upon his journal and the map. Haltingly, the trapper read the most recent entries aloud. Thus, they learned how the man met his death at the hands of the Indians. He also came across a notation in the journal requesting that anyone who might find it please deliver it to the businessman in St. Louis who had financed the expedition. Near the campfire they found the saddlebags containing the silver ingots.

Days later when the trappers returned to St. Louis, they turned the Frenchman's belongings, including the journal, over to the businessman. The businessman studied the journal and the map closely, contemplating the notion of financing another expedition into the Ozark Mountains in search of the rich silver mine. In the meantime, he learned about the growing threat of hostile Indians in the area of the mine and decided against it. One year later, the businessman turned the journal and the map over to a newspaper reporter. The following week, one of the St. Louis papers carried the story of the lost silver mine in the Ozarks.

The newspaper article also provided the directions to the mine taken from the journal. It described a fast-flowing creek not far from the mine that had its origins in a spring that poured out of a limestone bluff. The creek ran for some distance before joining a river that flowed from the southwest. From the point of the confluence of the river and the stream, the two men had traveled northwest for seven miles to a narrow, north-south oriented valley. From this valley, they rode up a ravine between two tall bluffs. Deep in this ravine was the lost silver mine.

Those who have studied this tale closely are convinced that the stream described is the Roaring River. Via the process of elimination, the larger river that flows from the southwest can only be the White River. Following the rest of the directions, the lost silver mine would be located a short distance south of the present day town of White Rock.

For another sixty to seventy years following the deaths of the two men who found the cave, Indian hostilities in the

Ozark Mountains inhibited or prevented additional searches. In time, the tale of the lost silver mine was largely forgotten. During the 1880s, someone came across a copy of the newspaper article that contained the story and a facsimile of the treasure map. Interest in the mine was rekindled, but the few searches that were undertaken were unsuccessful. It is possible that the fact that the two friends covered the entrance to the cave before leaving the area has foiled the attempts of those looking for it.

While the directions to the lost silver mine are clear and precise and should permit a searcher to arrive in the location of the cave, a significant obstacle has intruded into the process in recent years. The location described on the map and in the Frenchman's journal is today under the waters of Table Rock Lake.

Neosho Falls Treasure

Somewhere near a waterfall not far from the town of Neosho, Missouri, a box of jewels worth a fortune was buried some time during the last half for the nineteenth century. Directions to the lost treasure have been found, but to date this cache has not been recovered.

This intriguing tale has its origins across the Atlantic Ocean in Spain. During the year 1870, a young man and his new bride were moving into his family's ancestral home in the city of Toledo located in the central part of the country. Throughout the following weeks, the couple undertook the job of remodeling the home to suit their needs. While tearing down one wall in the house, the young man discovered an old snuff box that had been hidden within. Curious, he opened it and removed a weathered manuscript. He unfolded the document, laid it on the kitchen table, and by the light of a candle read an amazing account of lost treasure in the new world. It was signed by his grandfather.

Within the week, the young man took the manuscript to his mother and explained what it concerned, that it involved her father and his search for wealth in North America. As his mother prepared tea, she invited him to sit down with her as she told him about his grandfather and his quest.

The grandfather had been a soldier, and in that capacity had traveled much of the world from one Spanish possession to another. The occupation suited his zest for adventure, but in time being an officer in the Spanish army carried tedious responsibilities he was unwilling to shoulder. He resigned his commission and searched for other ways to satisfy his need for adventure. The grandfather had long been fascinated with the Spanish search for El Dorado, the mythical city of gold believed to exist in the New World and that had obsessed Coronado.

The grandfather sought and received financial backing and subsequently assembled a party of like-minded ex-soldiers and other men willing to accept a challenge. One of the backers provided the grandfather with a metal box containing a fortune in jewels, explaining they could be used to sell or trade for supplies and provisions along the way. The box, according to the manuscript, contained emeralds, pearls, rubies, and sapphires. The grandfather also had in his possession a map that had been constructed during the Coronado expedition three centuries earlier.

Months later, the party landed at a point near where the Mississippi River enters the Gulf of Mexico. While the ship lay at anchor and was tended by a small crew, the main party disembarked and rowed to shore. Three hundred miles and several days later, the grandfather led the group to a point where another large river entered the Mississippi. They followed it, traveling northwestward. This would have been the Arkansas River. They walked for several more days, eventually reaching Dardanelle Rocks. From here, they continued upriver for another one hundred miles where they turned northward and entered the southern realm of the Ozark Mountains. For the next fifteen days, they traveled on foot, making their way through mazes of canyons and ridges that sometimes doubled back onto each other. They made slow progress, and at times were forced to flee from hostile Indians living in the area.

On the evening of the fifteenth day, they made camp in a small valley that contained a waterfall. Here, they remained for several more days resting and hunting game. Since they had encountered no one with whom to trade for supplies and provisions, and because the box of jewels was relatively heavy, the grandfather thought it prudent to cache it until such time as it was needed. He searched around for a suitable hiding place. After finding one, he hid the jewels and marked the location.

The party of Spaniards spent months exploring this new land but found no El Dorado. In time, they returned to their ship anchored in the Gulf of Mexico. During their trek back to the vessel, they were unable to return to the location where the jewels were cached to retrieve them. The grandfather was determined to make a second journey to the area. At that time he would unearth the treasure and put it to the use for which it was intended.

When the grandfather returned to his home in Toledo, Spain, he wrote an account of his voyage and his search for wealth. It was this manuscript that the grandson found in the snuff box.

The grandson was intrigued with his grandfather's adventures. He was also interested in the metal box of jewels that had been buried at some remote location in the Ozark Mountains. Compelled by the story and the promise of wealth, he began to make plans to travel to America to find the box of jewels.

He read the manuscript many times, almost to the point of knowing it by heart. In particular, he turned time and again to the passage that described the location where the jewels were buried. The Spanish distances were translated into miles for purposes of clarity.

> Proceed up the river called the Mississippi beyond where it is joined by the Red River, thence up the Arkansas River to the promontory known as Dardanelle Rocks. Passing this point, proceed another one hundred miles upriver. From here, travel overland due north for fifteen days to an area wherein is located a waterfall, the only one to be found. At a point halfway between the falls and a small creek to the north will be found a large flat rock with an arrow carved upon the surface. From this rock, walk ninety paces due east, the direction in which the arrow is pointed. Then, walk ten paces south. The box of jewelry is buried here.

Person may have changed direction arrow is facing, so E is wrong.

The young man traveled to America in 1880, determined to locate the metal box filled with jewels. It would have been worth a fortune, and he and his wife would be able to live in luxury for the rest of their lives.

He traveled alone. His trip across the Atlantic Ocean on a ship was uneventful. On landing near the city of New Orleans, he purchased a horse and pack mule, loaded up on provisions, and followed the Mississippi River upstream to its confluence with the Arkansas River. This portion of the trip was likewise without note. He passed the Dardanelle Rocks, to this day a prominent landmark in Arkansas. After proceeding another one hundred miles upriver as indicated in his grandfather's manuscript, he turned north and entered the Ozark Mountains.

Once into the mountain range, he suffered the same consequences as did his grandfather. He became lost time and again trying to make his way through the valleys and over the ridges. He wandered around for days, disoriented and lost. He exhausted his provisions and was forced to live off the land. Never an adept outdoorsman, he was unable to bring down game and for days subsisted on wild grapes, berries, and onions. After weeks of travel, he finally arrived at the small valley described by his grandfather. He set up a camp. He harvested more wild plants and was successful at snaring a rabbit. He rested for several days, stirring only to search for the flat stone upon which was carved an arrow.

One afternoon he found it. He followed his grandfather's directions closely, but after several attempts was never able to locate the site where the metal box of jewels was buried. Remembering that his grandfather was a short man, the grandson adjusted his paces in the hope that they matched. Still, he could not find the jewels. Discouraged, he gave up and returned to Spain. He never again ventured to America to search for the treasure.

Following the directions provided in the old manuscript, and making adjustments for time as a result of unfamiliarity with the terrain, one will eventually arrive at a small valley in the Missouri Ozarks. The valley contains a waterfall. The nearest town is Neosho and the name given to the waterfall is Neosho Falls. A short distance to the north of the waterfall is Turkey Creek. Somewhere between Neosho Falls and Turkey Creek lies the flat stone with the image of an arrow scratched onto its surface.

Since many years have passed between the time the grandfather made the mark on the stone and when the grandson arrived to search for the jewels, any one of several pertinent events could have transpired to thwart the search. It is possible that the growth of the surrounding vegetation, including briars and vines, could have covered the flat stone. If the stone was located near one wall of the valley, there exists the potential that it might have been covered up by a rockslide.

The consensus of those who have studied this tale of lost treasure is that the box of jewels is still there. Finding it may be a function of finding the flat stone with the arrow. If the metal box was not buried deep, the possibility of locating it with a metal detector is great.

Letter Shows Way to Lost Treasure

Somewhere not far from the city of Springfield is a cave that allegedly contains a large Spanish treasure. Mystery surrounds this tale. No one has any knowledge of the source of this great treasure, and it remains unclear how it came to be in this place. The exact location of the cave has never been determined.

In the year 1932, a prominent Springfield family came into possession of a letter describing a huge Spanish treasure that had been hidden in a cave a short distance from the city. The letter was written in Spanish and mailed from Mexico. It was never explained why the letter was sent to Springfield, and the family never revealed the source.

The letter was originally penned on May 10, 1848, in the Mexican town of Delverte. None of the family members read or spoke Spanish, so they hired someone to translate for them. For reasons never explained, the contents of the letter were published in a July 1935 edition of the *Springfield News and Leader*. It is reproduced here word for word and no attempt has been made to correct grammar or structure.

Go to what is now called Springfield. Greene County, Missouri. It is a village about twenty miles up the James River above the old Spanish town of Levarro. Leave the James River and go to Springfield. It has an open square in the center. There is an old road or trail that leaves from the southwest corner of the square and runs southwest.

Follow this trail for about two-and-one-half miles. You will come to a dim road running east and west. Go west on this road about a half-mile and you will come to a big spring, some big timber, and two or three old cabins.

If you look carefully, you will find some sinks in the ground about four hundred paces southwest of the big spring, and across the creek there is a bluff. About three hundred paces from the center of the bluff and down the creek, there is another spring, not so large as the first. Somewhere near the center of the bluff, and fronting north on the creek, was the main entrance to the cave. It was filled up and covered by a big stone and there are three turkey tracks carved on the stone in a straight line east and west, and two of the same above. Remove this stone and also the filling for twelve or thirteen feet, and you will find a passage that descends for about twelve feet. When you reach the bottom of this descent, you will find a passage bearing nearly south. A little further on you will find one running southwest. This is a false passage about thirty feet in length. It was cut to reach a deeper passage coming under the creek from the south side. It was abandoned when the new entrance was made.

The one you follow is the one running nearly south and dips down. You follow this until you enter a large room being used to work as a smelter to make bullion and Spanish money. The tools are there. My father and brother worked there years ago, and they have taken some from there after the Spanish left that country. There is plenty more for a dozen people, and more in sight.

If you cannot find it by these directions, you follow the creek that runs through Springfield and runs southwest. Follow it out to the flat or bottom where you will find a big spring, and just beyond the big spring about three hundred paces there is another creek coming into this creek a little north of the east bluff where the cave is, dividing this bluff opposite the big spring and the bluff where the creek runs together. The creek here runs a little south of west.

I think the entrance to the mines was near the center of the bluff, on the north side, fronting the creek and above high water. When you leave the east and west dim road, there are three large oak trees. They are marked: The first tree is marked with a turkey foot; the second tree with two turkey feet; the third tree has two turkey feet cut on the north side of the tree and pointing south by west. The spring is on the south side of the creek. Four hundred and ninety-six paces from the spring, southwest on the south side of the creek, is the entrance to the mines on the north side of the bluff near the creek.

Be patient and you will find it as the above is described.

There are three kegs of gold stored in a niche in the big room, covered with gravel and broken bones.

José, if you succeed in finding this, be on your guard as to Saville.

The family that received the mysterious letter claimed no knowledge of any hidden treasure. Further, they claimed no connection to anyone Spanish or Mexican whatsoever. They were unaware of anyone named José or any person or place named Saville.

In an odd circumstance, a second letter arrived at the home of another Springfield family in 1937. This letter was originally written some time in the 1890s. It was of handwriting different from the first, but provides essentially the same directions to the treasure cave. The description of the treasure corresponds exactly with that found in the first letter.

Then, in 1939 yet another letter surfaced. Like the others, this one provided directions to the treasure cave, the mines, and a description of the cache. The letter had somehow come into the possession of two men who were searching for the treasure cave. Following the directions in the third letter, they claimed, they found the cave. They removed the stone covering the opening and dug through the fill dirt. The interior of the cave matched the descriptions in the letters. Though they searched the cave for several days, they found no treasure. They did note, however, that some of the passageways had been closed off as a result of cave-ins.

Over the years, several have searched for the treasure cave using the directions provided in the letters. Like the two men who claimed to have located the cave in 1939, others likewise have announced finding it. And like the two before them, described the rock-choked passageways that allegedly lead to the treasure cache.

In 1999, an assessment was made of the conditions in the cave by a civil engineer who was hired by an anonymous employer. While he was exploring the cave, the engineer said he found several old and rusted tools of apparent ancient origin. He suspected they had belonged to the Spanish who once worked there. He also substantiated the previous observations in his report that at least three passageways were blocked by cave-ins. The limestone rock at this location, he wrote, was very old and brittle. He recommended that if any recovery process was undertaken, that great care be exercised in shoring up the cave to inhibit or limit the potential for cave-in.

Yet another mystery associated with this tale is the identity of the person who hired the engineer. The investigation and report is suggestive of the notion that someone intended to make an attempt at removing the fill from previous cave-ins and retrieving the treasure. Two years after the assessment was made by the engineer, a road was bladed into the area that is the presumed location of the treasure cave. To date, however, no announcement of a treasure find has been made.

Bear Hollow
near Lanagan

Thirty Bags of Gold

Some time during the year 1884, a stranger arrived in the small town of Lanagan, Missouri. He checked into the only hotel and from time to time was seen eating supper in the town's café. The stranger spent the day exploring areas outside of town as if searching for something. Those who encountered him on these explorations claimed that the stranger often referred to a map.

One evening as the newcomer was eating supper, a Lanagan resident paused by his table, introduced himself, and welcomed him to the area. The stranger invited the resident to sit with him. He introduced himself and said he had lived in many places, most recently Mexico. He gave his name as Van Wormer, and the two men entered into a prolonged conversation that involved a strange tale of lost treasure.

In the newcomer's possession was a map. It was clearly very old, drawn and notated on parchment, and purported to show the location of thirty bags of gold that had been buried nearby over one hundred years earlier. During the conversation, the stranger asked the resident about local landmarks and other features that he needed to understand in order to properly interpret the map.

The resident provided what information he knew. When he asked the stranger how he came into possession of the map, the newcomer remained vague and tried to change the subject. Eventually, he explained the tale behind the treasure.

During the first half of the 1700s, a party of Mexican miners was making its way through the Ozark Mountains on the way to New Orleans. They were transporting thirty bags of gold. Where the gold came from and where the miners had been prior to entering the Ozarks remains a mystery. On approaching a place known today as Bear Hollow, the Mexicans were attacked by Indians. The Mexicans defended themselves as best they could, but they were outnumbered and unfamiliar with the terrain. They succeeded in repelling the attack, but half of their number was killed. Most of the pack animals were dead or wounded, thus they were unable to transport the gold any further.

When the sun had set, the Indians pulled back and set up camp. The Mexicans could see their campfire in the distance and presumed they were waiting for dawn to launch another attack. Concerned that the Indians were after the gold, the Mexicans decided they should hide it and try to make an escape during the night. They carried the thirty bags of gold to an adjacent canyon wall and stuffed them into a crevice. They then filled the opening with rocks and forest debris.

Following the caching of the treasure, they hastily buried their dead comrades. Leaving what few horses remained alive, they crept away on foot. They managed to elude the Indians and by dawn were several miles away. They made plans to travel to New Orleans, recruit a contingent of armed men, and return for the gold. Nothing, however, was ever heard from the party of Mexicans again.

Van Wormer told his visitor that in his searches he found some of the graves of the Mexicans that had been killed by the Indians. He claimed he had dug into them and discovered enough artifacts to prove their identity.

The map in the possession of Van Wormer was unclear about the location of the niche where the bags of gold had been cached. He also observed that considerable erosion of the soft limestone rock that makes up this part of the Ozark Mountains had taken place. Furthermore, he said, occasional floods and at least one forest fire had modified the hollow to the degree that it bore scant resemblance to what had been sketched on the map.

Van Wormer spent another two weeks searching for the treasure, but was unable to find it. At the end of that time, he packed up, checked out of the hotel, and was never seen again.

In 1928, the town of Lanagan received another visitor. Like Van Wormer, this one possessed a map purporting to show the location of thirty bags of gold hidden by a party of Mexicans during the early 1700s. Also like Van Wormer, this man spent most of his days in Bear Hollow.

During his stay, it was learned that the newcomer was the son of Van Wormer. Though like his father, he was vague about how his family had come into possession of the treasure map, he freely related the story of how the treasure came to be hidden in the nearby hollow.

After many days of searching, however, the young Van Wormer was unable to locate the gold. He departed the area, never to return. Some who visited Bear Hollow in the wake of his departure found several shallow excavations and a camp site.

The lure of the thirty bags of gold cached in Bear Hollow remains. Treasure hunters familiar with the tale come to the area with hopes of finding it, but so far it continues to elude the searchers.

Pending on height & slope on top of canyon wall, could be covered in debris and require digging to locate (or, just a deep detector run over all canyon wall bases at an angle).

It'd represent a huge surface area to detect, so shouldn't be a problem.

or might be in a crevice not directly under/at base, but in wall of canyon.

Sinkhole Treasure

Fifteen miles south of the town of West Plains and just a short distance north of the Arkansas border lies a buried treasure consisting of silverware, jewelry, pocket watches, and 1,200 gold coins taken during Confederate raids. The location was described by a dying man who was involved with caching the loot. The treasure is still there.

In 1913, a seventy-seven year old man lay dying in a Kansas City hospital. During one of his lucid moments, he called out to a nurse and told her he needed to talk to someone immediately, that he had information about a cache of stolen treasure. The nurse was busy with her rounds and no doctors were available, so she went to an adjacent room and asked a patient named Tom Hoots to come and hear the dying man's story. Hoots agreed. He seated himself next to the old man's bed, introduced himself, and told him that he would listen to what he had to say. What Tom Hoots heard that day was a most amazing tale of lost treasure.

The old man said his name was Henry Williams. He said that fifty years earlier he had been working in a livery in

Pocahontas, Arkansas, when nine hundred Confederate troops under the command of Colonel Joseph Porter arrived. The soldiers set up camp just outside of town and began making preparations to launch a raid on Federal troops in Missouri. The Missouri border was about twenty straight-line miles to the north.

Williams didn't care for the Confederate soldiers. He said they were rude to the residents of the town and picked fights with adult males who were not serving in the military. In addition, Williams didn't like his job in the stables; he was earning only four dollars a week. He said he decided to leave Pocahontas for someplace where he would feel more comfortable and perhaps make a little more money.

When Williams learned that Porter and his troops were going to head north and west, he packed his few personal belongings onto his two mules and set out on the trail ahead of them. It led to the small town of Franklin, Arkansas. Williams thought the settlers in the area had gotten word of Porter's advancing army and might have fled for safety. He intended to see if he could locate anything valuable on the abandoned farms.

By the end of the first day of travel Williams had covered about fifteen miles. He led his mules to a grove of trees to set up camp and found three men already there, each with a mule. Several leather bags were lying by their campfire. Williams introduced himself and the three men told him they were from Walnut Ridge, Arkansas. They had been traveling for several days, but because of the heavy loads their mules were going lame.

Since Williams didn't possess much, he offered to carry some of the men's bags on his own pack animals. As the three strangers separated their belongings for the repacking,

Williams learned they possessed more than 3,000 pieces of silverware, some jewelry, pocket watches, 470 silver dollars, and $19,000 in gold coins. Though Williams did not ask the men how they happened to come by such riches, he presumed it was stolen.

The next afternoon when they entered Franklin, the town was abuzz with the news that thousands of Confederate soldiers were on the way there and planned on looting the town. Most of the population of sixty had already loaded their possessions into wagons and fled. The four men looked around for some food, but were unable to find any. Williams said he learned later that the Confederates had bypassed Franklin without causing any harm.

From Franklin, Williams and his companions turned north and traveled a short distance to Pilot Hill. They remained in camp for two weeks as they tried to ascertain the route taken by Porter and his men. From time to time they foraged about in the countryside searching for recently abandoned homesteads where they might find some food.

One of their treks took them back to Franklin where they learned that Porter's command was still in Pocahontas and would not leave until December 2. All the while the four remained in camp it rained and the temperature had fallen. Though they were bored and miserable, they were grateful for the chance to give their mules some rest. They made plans to travel to West Plains and Houston, Missouri. They assumed that since most of the residents in those towns were Yankee sympathizers, they would flee on hearing that Porter's men were approaching. Williams and his companions intended to loot the homes.

On the day they broke camp and headed north, they encountered the body of a Union soldier just off the trail.

Would a d. map show a sinkhole Research

Williams removed the uniform from the dead man and placed it in his own pack in case he might need it later.

On December 4, they entered the tiny village of Sturkie, Arkansas. On arriving, they told everyone they encountered that the Confederates were heading this way. They watched as the panicking citizens loaded wagons and rode out of town. The four men then casually looted homes and stores, and in this manner they acquired $900 in coins and some decent bedding.

Just before leaving Sturkie, Williams donned the Yankee uniform as protection against the worsening cold. Four-and-one-half miles north of the town, they paused at a spring and allowed time for their mules to drink their fill. Just as they were preparing to depart, they heard the sound of a barking dog. It was getting closer. Not wanting to be found, the men led their mules into the nearby dense forest. About 400 yards from the spring they encountered a sinkhole. They paused here and peered through the trees back in the direction of the barking dog.

Within a few minutes the barking became louder. Then, the dog bounded into sight around a bend in the trail. Close behind were four Confederate troopers on horseback. Williams presumed this was Porter's advance guard. Fearing the consequences should they be caught with so much treasure, they decided to hide it. Peering into the sinkhole, they spotted a tiny cave they thought would be an ideal hiding place. Unfortunately it turned out to be too small and too difficult to reach. Instead, the four men excavated a shallow trench along one side of the sinkhole and buried the treasure.

Moments later, the four troopers, following the tracks of the mules, rode up to the four men with drawn weapons and arrested them. According to Williams, the Rebel soldiers appeared to be more interested in the mules than they were in the men. As they entered into a discussion as to what to do with the prisoners and the stock, a shot rang out and one of them crumpled to the ground, dead.

An instant later, twelve Union soldiers rode up, surrounded them, and took all of their weapons. This done, Williams, his friends, and the three remaining Confederates were marched to a nearby spring. It is known today as Lost Spring.

Wasting no time, the Yankee soldiers prepared to hang the three men who had been with Williams. William's assumed he was spared because he was wearing a Union uniform. As nooses were being prepared, one of the Confederate soldiers bolted for the woods. He was shot down in seconds. Following this, his two comrades were strung up.

Williams thought he was going to be next when a Union officer stepped up and began questioning him and asking why he was wearing the uniform of the north. Williams, thinking quickly, told the officer he had been on a scouting mission for General Marmaduke's command and had been taken prisoner by the three men. He also told him he knew about Porter's bivouac near Pocahontas.

As a result of William's story, the Yankee officer was convinced of his innocence. His mules and belongings were returned to him and he was invited to accompany the Yankee soldiers to the town of West Plains. There, he was assigned to help three families drive their wagons to safety at Rolla, 120 miles away.

During the trip, Williams thought constantly about the treasure buried back near the sinkhole and wondered when he would have an opportunity to return for it. He realized he was the only man left alive who knew of the existence of the treasure.

Two days after reaching Rolla, Williams was ordered to go to Knobview, and then on to St. Louis. By now he was earning his living as a Union solider. In 1863, he was transferred to the Illinois infantry at Evansville where his assignment was to guard the riverfront.

From his bed and with great difficulty, Williams related the entire story behind the lost treasure near the sinkhole. He told Hoots that he thought about it every day but something always prevented him from returning to it.

Exhausted from the telling, Henry Williams laid back on his pillow. In a few moments he told Hoots he was having trouble breathing. Then, he went into a coughing fit. A minute later he was dead.

Hoots didn't place much credence in the story related by Henry Williams. One year later, he purchased a farm not far from West Plains. With the passage of some time, Hoots began to research some aspects of Williams' tale. He met some people who were related to the families from the small wagon train Williams escorted from West Plains to Rolla. Though they did not remember Williams, they verified a number of aspects of the story.

In 1914, Tom Hoots moved to Archie, Missouri, where he found a job with the postal service. His son remained on the farm in West Plains. Having heard the story of Henry Williams' buried treasure many times from his father, the son became interested in locating it. Following several searches, he located the sinkhole and Lost Spring. Everything was just as Williams had described it.

The Hoots son, along with two friends, returned to the site and began digging near the sinkhole. Hoots realized he had no information related to how near or far from the sinkhole the treasure had been cached. On the fourth day of digging, several pieces of silverware were found. Though they worked for another full day, however, no other treasure was located.

The younger Hoots returned to the site several times to dig for the treasure but it continued to elude him. Eventually, he abandoned his quest to find the cache.

During the period of time when the younger Hoots was searching for the cache of gold and silver coins and silverware, high-tech metal detectors were not available. Had they been, his search might have been much easier. By the time such equipment had become available and affordable, Hoots passed away.

The treasure, worth a fortune today, still lies just below the surface of the ground near the sinkhole and Lost Spring.

The Tilley Treasure

Wilson M. Tilley was a successful farmer who lived on a huge parcel of land not far from the present-day town of Waynesville located between Rolla and Lebanon, Missouri. Tilley raised cattle and crops and occasionally traded and sold horses. Though he was one of the wealthiest residents of the area, he was known as a miser. He purchased new clothes only when his old ones were little more than rags. When he did make a purchase, he argued and negotiated with the storekeeper until the poor man was willing to sell the items at any price just to get rid of Tilley.

Tilley cared little for banks and never set foot in one. Instead, he hid his money at some secret location on his farm. When Tilley conducted business, he always insisted he be paid in silver coins. He refused to accept paper currency, stating that it was worthless.

It is also believed by many that Tilley amassed a large amount of money during the Civil War. As a result of fluctuating land and money values, Tilley indulged in speculation, often securing a piece of property at a low rate and then selling it when the value rose. It was said Tilley took advantage of families that were unable to keep up the payments on their farms.

One day Tilley was visited by a banker who invited him to open an account at his institution. Tilley laughed at the visitor, telling him that he didn't consider banks to be safe. He cited several examples of area banks being robbed by outlaws. He told the banker that his money, all coins, was buried in four wooden chests at a location known only to him and that no one would ever be able to find it.

During the War, Tilley was a known Southern sympathizer. One afternoon, a gang of mounted Union bushwackers rode onto his farm, entered his house, and dragged him out into the yard. They told him they were aware of his fortune and demanded he turn it over to them. When Tilley refused, they subjected him to a severe beating, then threatened to set fire to his house and barn. Still, the farmer would not reveal the secret hiding place of his fortune.

Growing impatient, the bushwackers told Tilley he had one last chance to tell them where his money was hidden or they would hang him. Tilley continued to refuse, telling the bushwackers they would have to find it for themselves.

At a signal from the leader, one of the gang fastened a noose in a length of rope and tossed it over the branch of a nearby tree. Two others tied Tilley's hands behind his back and lifted him to the back of a horse. After the noose was placed around his neck and tightened, the leader approached and asked once again about the location of the money. It was said that Tilley spat at him. With that, the horse was quirted. Tilley was yanked from the saddle by the rope and swung like a pendulum until he choked to death several minutes later.

The bushwackers looted the house. They searched for Tilley's treasure but were never able to find it. Finally, they rode away. Tilley was found two days later, cut down, and buried. During successive years, tales about the lost Tilley treasure spread throughout that part of Missouri. Occasionally someone would arrive at the old Tilley farm and search about for the cache, sometimes digging holes in the yard. Nothing was ever found.

Years passed, and the Tilley treasure was all but forgotten when a significant event took place. Four miles south of Waynesville near Route H in 1962, a bulldozer was clearing some land not far from the old Tilley property. After making a pass across a slight slope, the dozer operator noticed that the blade had uncovered an object. Curious, he climbed down to inspect it.

What he encountered were two wooden boxes. The blade had torn the tops from them revealing their contents. Both boxes were filled to the top with silver coins including dimes, quarters, half-dollars, and silver dollars. The dates on the coins ranged from 1841 to 1862.

The discovery was the most talked-about topic for the next several weeks throughout the area. Everyone was convinced that the dozer operator uncovered the long-lost Tilley treasure. At least part of it, anyway.

It soon became apparent that the two boxes of coins represented only half of the Tilley fortune. In no time at all, the newly cleared land was swarming with people who had come from the surrounding area as well as from other states. Campsites were set up and searchers ranged across the property inspecting any likely site. Holes were dug but nothing was ever found. Eventually the owner of the property, weary of the commotion and the trespassing, had the county sheriff evict the searchers.

In the half-century since the discovery of half of the Tilley treasure, a few others have attempted to locate the remainder. Armed with state-of-the-art metal detectors, some have searched the area where the first find took place but to date have found nothing.

When Tilley spoke of his buried treasure cache, he referred to it as only one place. Many suspect that remaining two boxes of buried coins will be found near the location where the previous two were unearthed. One researcher is certain he knows where they are. He suggests that when Tilley buried them, he cached them all together with the boxes stacked two deep. When the dozer operator uncovered the two boxes in 1962, he claimed, he was unaware that the remaining two boxes were under the ones he removed.

There are others familiar with the tale of the Tilley treasure who agree with this contention. The only problem is, no one remembers where the first two boxes were found. Furthermore, the remaining boxes of coins may be just deep enough that they are out of the depth range for most metal detectors.

Lost Box of Gold Coins

During the years 1849 and 1850, men from the eastern and southern United States traveled westward to California by the thousands. Responding to the news that gold could be found in abundance in and around the Sacramento River and the Sierra Nevada Mountains, many left homes, farms, and families in search of wealth. Some made respectable fortunes, but many returned to their origins broke and broken. Others found wealth in unexpected places.

One of those was Tom Livingston. Livingston was from Tennessee and like many others was lured by the promise of riches in California. Livingston packed what little he owned onto a mule, saddled his horse, and joined the migration. His westward route, like that of many others, took him through Missouri.

Running low on provisions, Livingston rode into the bustling community of Joplin. As he purchased some beans and corn meal at a local mercantile, Livingston heard news of the productive lead mines that had been recently opened up in the area. Needing money, he applied for work at one of them and was hired the same day. Livingston figured to work for two weeks, collect enough cash to make more progress on his westward journey.

Livingston was no stranger to mining. As a boy, he had worked for a time in the copper mines in Tennessee. Livingston was a large man, burly and muscular, and it was nothing for him to put in a twelve hour day in the mines. He was not only a good worker, he was interested in all aspects of the mining operation and did not hesitate to ask questions. In this manner, he learned that the lead had been mined in this area on a small scale for more than a hundred years. The local Indians knew about the deposits, and they told the Spanish explorers who arrived in the 1600s as well as the French trappers who came during the 1700s. When white settlers arrived in significant numbers during the 1800s, many of them found outcrops of lead in the nearby Ozark Mountains.

The lead was mined and used specifically for molding bullets. Initially, men would retrieve the lead when they ran short of ammunition. By the time Livingston arrived in Joplin, the demand for lead caused residents to take the mining operations more seriously. The lead was abundant, prices were up, and the demand was high. Several lead mines had been opened and production was high. Realizing the prospects for making money were as likely here in the Missouri Ozarks as in the California Sierras, Livingston decided to start his own lead mine.

Livingston worked long enough to acquire a decent grubstake. He set out to explore the Ozark Mountains and within two weeks discovered a rich vein of lead. The vein appeared to be endless, and mixed in with the lead was silver and zinc. By the time four months had passed, Livingston's lead mine was in full operation and he had in his employ nearly one hundred men. Nearby, he started a town he named Minersville. A short time later, Livingston located another significant lead vein a few miles away and developed it. Another town named Leadville sprouted in the vicinity. Both Minersville and Leadville are ghost towns today.

Livingston's two mines were highly productive and made impressive profits from the beginning. By the late 1850s, Livingston had become one of the wealthiest men in southwestern Missouri. By this time he had a wife and family. Life was good, the profits continued to roll in, and Livingston wanted for little. Then, southwestern Missouri received news of the outbreak of the Civil War.

Being a Tennessean, Livingston held strong Southern sympathies. In southwestern Missouri he was surrounded by a mix of advocates of the Confederacy as well as anti-slavery forces. Both the Union and the Confederacy were in need of lead for bullets, and Livingston was determined his output would find its way only to the Rebels.

One morning Livingston was involved with some paperwork at the mine office in Leadville when a worker informed him that a contingent of mounted Union troopers was approaching. The rumor in town was that the Yankees were going to take over the mine.

Defiant, Livingston was determined that would not happen. He hurried outside and assembled his miners. He instructed them to gather up all of the lead that had been accumulated from recent mining activities and dump it in the nearby creek. Wagons were loaded with the ore, mules were hitched up, and the wagons driven to the creek. As the last of the lead was dumped into the stream, the Union soldiers were seen riding up the trail.

Livingston suspected that if he were captured he would be hanged or imprisoned. He decided escape was his only alternative. He dashed back to his office. From under his desk he pulled a metal box containing over $10,000 in gold

Near IR to locate trail?

coins. He placed the box in the back of one of the wagons, leapt onto the seat, and whipped the mule team down a road that led from the mines to the town of Minersville.

Almost a week passed with no word from Livingston. His wife expressed concern that he may have been overtaken and killed. Then, she received a letter from the miner. In his missive, he stated that he was going to join the Confederate army and dedicate his life to fighting the Yankees. He also told his wife that just before arriving in Minersville during his escape, he stopped long enough to bury the metal box filled with gold coins. He said he buried it a few feet off the trail next to a rock that was shaped like a buffalo. He explained that when he returned home from the War, he would dig up the gold and use the money to reopen his lead mines.

Nothing more was ever heard from Tom Livingston and his fate remains a mystery. His wife attempted to trace him during the War but with no success. When the fighting was over, she invested time, energy, and money into learning what became of him, but information was never forthcoming.

Following the War, several of Livingston's miners took over the mines but eventually sold them for a total of $100. One hundred years later, the same mines produced more than fifty million dollars worth of lead with no end in sight.

The buried metal box filled with gold coins became the object of a search by Livingston's wife. With one of her sons, she traveled the road from the mine to the town of Minersville looking for a rock shaped like a buffalo. She encountered hundred of rocks and boulders, but not the one for which she searched. After two years she finally gave up.

Others, learning of the story of Livingston's buried cache, came to search for it but like the miner's wife, could never find it.

During the 1970s, a weekend hiker was exploring around what remains of the Minersville ghost town. He poked among the ruins of the old buildings and collected a few antique bottles. He also took several photographs. Three weeks later he visited a friend who lived in Joplin and knew the story of Tom Livingston's lost gold cache. As the friend examined the photographs from the recent visit to Minersville, he paused at one of an odd-shaped rock. Examining it closely, he saw that it was about three feet tall and resembled a buffalo. He asked where the photograph was taken. The weekend hiker could not remember exactly, but it was among those that were shot at or near Minersville. The friend then related the story of Livingston's lost coins.

The following weekend, the two men traveled to the area in hopes of relocating the rock. The possibility of finding Livingston's buried treasure was uppermost in their minds and they regarded their chances as excellent. On arriving at Minersville, however, they were unable to find the buffalo-shaped rock.

At least three others were shown the photograph. Each traveled to the region to try to find the rock, but it eluded them also. That Livingston's fortune in gold is buried next to this rock is not in question. The main problem with recovering the treasure is related to finding the rock. It is there, the photographs prove it. It is estimated that the buried gold would be worth in excess of one-half million dollars today.

Lost Posthole Banks

For many years during and after the Civil War, the nation's financial situation remained unstable and unpredictable. Banks went out of business regularly even while new ones were being established. To make matters worse, the growing number of bank robberies following the War further placed depositors' money in jeopardy. Thus, it came as no surprise that many hid their savings on their own property.

A popular hiding place was behind a loose stone in the hearth. Others hid coins and currency beneath floorboards, behind walls, and sometimes simply placed it inside crockery that remained in plain sight. A less common location for caching money, but one favored by many, was what has come to be called a "posthole bank."

The method is simple. A fence post would be pulled up and a Mason jar or coffee can containing coins and/or currency was placed in the hole and the post reset. Corner posts were favored because they were easy to remember. Many early settlers went to their graves without leaving directions to their posthole banks. As a result, uncountable fortunes still remain in the ground a few inches below the surface where they were cached years ago.

One such posthole banker was a man named Ed Henson. Henson owned a farm near Unionville, Missouri, the seat of Putnam County. Henson, like many of his neighbors, was distrustful of banks and refused to deposit his money in one. Over the years, Henson earned a decent income from farming. It was also said he had an interest in a sawmill and a freighting company. Over the years, when Henson did business, he preferred to be paid in silver coins. As a result, he accumulated a significant fortune for the times in silver dollars. When family members asked him where he kept his wealth, he refused to tell them.

When Ed Henson died in 1949, family members searched for days for a will but could not find one. It was a fact that Henson had accumulated tens of thousands of dollars in coins over the years. It was also a fact that he hid them in some location on his property. Though family members searched for weeks, his money was never found.

Several months following the death of Ed Henson, his property was sold and the new owners set about renovating the house and barn. A formal survey showed that Henson's fence line on the western edge of the property was located almost eight feet inside the true boundary. As a result, the old fence was torn down and a new one placed in the proper location.

The new owner of the Henson property had occupied the place for eighteen months when he made an important discovery. As he was cleaning old and unwanted materials from the barn he encountered several coffee cans filled with nails, screws, and other hardware. One of the cans he picked up appeared to be empty, but when he was about to discard it he spotted something stuffed inside. With great care, he removed a piece of paper that had been folded many times. He unfolded it and in the light of the open barn door saw that it contained writing in pencil. On close examination, he realized it was the last will and testament of Ed Henson.

The owner immediately contacted Henson's relatives who were living in Unionville. When they arrived at the house the following day, they read the will and discovered that Henson had buried close to $40,000 in silver coins in coffee cans and Mason jars in posthole banks related to the fence on the western boundary. Relieved at receiving this information, the family made plans to retrieve the caches when they were informed by the new owner that the old fence had been pulled up and a new one built. Furthermore, he explained, that portion of the farm had been plowed and seeded and no evidence of the old fence line existed.

The Henson relatives insisted on visiting the site. On arriving, they examined the ground for some distance inside the old fence line but were unable to discern the location of the old postholes. A few exploratory holes were dug but nothing was recovered. Dejected, the family members returned to town.

The Henson property changed hands at least three times during the next fifty years. During the 1960s, the owner at the time planted the west field in corn. One day in 1964, he arrived in Unionville with an amazing story. He said he had been plowing his field near the fence when the blade kicked up something from the ground. Curious, the farmer climbed down off of his tractor to inspect it. To his astonishment, it was a coffee can filled to the top with old silver dollars. Between the real and antique value, it was estimated to be worth $10,000.

The discovery set off a spate of renewed interest in Henson's lost posthole banks. The farmer plowed over the area several timers but was unable to unearth any more caches. One morning he arrived at his field and found that someone had entered the property during the night and dug several holes. Clearly, he considered, they were searching for the caches.

Though many have searched for the remainder of Ed Henson's fortune over the years, it has not been found. Most who have researched this tale are convinced that the cans and jars filled with silver coins still lie beneath a few inches of soil several feet inside the fence line on the western edge of the property.

Lost Treasure of Dimes

One of the oddest lost treasures in Missouri history is that associated with a shipment of coins from Pennsylvania to California. It never made it to the intended destination and remains lost at the site of an Indian attack in 1850.

A little known historical fact is that almost all of the ten-cent pieces minted in 1844 disappeared. A total of 72,500 of them were made in the Philadelphia mint. Today, there are only a few left and these are in less than a dozen coin collections in the country. What happened to the rest of the dimes has been documented. The mystery relates to where they are.

Following the migration of tens of thousands of hopeful gold-seekers to California in 1849 and 1850, an acute shortage of change hampered business at retail locations throughout much of the northern part of the Golden State. A number of California banks banded together and petitioned the United States treasury to ship them a supply of change as soon as possible.

The coins—nickels, dimes, quarters, and silver dollars – were packed into a number of wooden boxes, labeled appropriately, and loaded into a boxcar. The train carried the coins to St. Louis where they were unloaded onto wagons and transferred to a boat. The boat steamed up a short portion of the Missouri before docking at a location called Westport Landing where they were transferred to wagons. The vehicles containing the coins were to accompany a wagon train enroute to California. According to the records, the dimes were placed in one wagon, silver dollars in another, and the quarters and nickels in yet another.

The following morning the train, including the wagons transporting the coins, departed Westport Landing. The coin-filled wagons, under guard, rode at the end of the procession. The day began quiet as the long train rumbled westward. Just before noon, a cry of alarm went up as the wagon train was attacked by Indians. The attack was launched at the front of the train, and all men who bore arms rushed forward to help with the defense. Within minutes, the entire crew, along with four passengers, was killed.

At the rear of the train, the drivers of the wagons containing the coins attempted to turn the vehicles and race back to Westport Landing. Two of the wagons succeeded in making the turn. The drivers whipped the teams hard and they were soon on their way to safety. The third wagon, the one transporting the dimes, became stuck during the turn. As the driver and a guard jumped down to try to free the vehicle, they were set upon by Indians and slain.

A handful of Indians leaped into the wagon and searched it for anything of value. Having no use for the money of the white man and finding little else of use in the wagon, they set it afire.

An hour later the Indians rode away, carrying with them whatever they found of value. Save for a handful of survivors who fled into a nearby grove of trees at the first warning of attack, all members of the wagon train were killed. Every wagon was set afire, and as the Indians disappeared to the north, the smoke rose high in the air.

Later that afternoon, the two wagons carrying the remaining coins arrived back at Westport. Here, they informed authorities of the attack on the train. Since Westport was a small settlement, there was little that could be done other than to try to travel to nearby St. Louis and organize a party of men to return to the scene. Because of the logistical difficulties, it was two days before the massacre site was revisited.

On finally arriving, they found a long line of burnt wagons. Anything not carried away by the Indians was destroyed. Bodies of the wagon train victims littered the landscape. A few had been scalped. Two men, a woman, and a child, on spotting the rescue party, emerged from the copse of trees to the south.

Little remained of the wagons save for ash, metal fittings, and charred bits of wood. The wagon transporting the 72,000 ten-cent pieces could not be identified and the boxes containing the coins were never found. The authorities mistakenly concluded that the Indians carried away the coins, thus a search for them was not undertaken.

The Indians had no use for the money. They would have found the heavy boxes of coins difficult to transport on horseback and hardly worth the effort. Instead, researchers believe, the coins, likely fused together as a result of the heat of the burning wagon and no doubt laid on the ground in a misshapen mass. It is possible that the rescuers rode by them and did not recognize them for what they were.

The dimes were never recovered. At least, not all of them. In 1895, a visitor to the massacre site found a heavy, dirt-encrusted, fist-sized lump of odd shape and configuration. Curious, he took it home, cleaned it, and discovered the lump consisted of dozens of ten-cent pieces that had been melted together. This, he concluded, was part of the original shipment of coins lost during the massacre. The rest of the coins no doubt melted together in one or more heavy masses. The finder was determined to return to the site and locate them.

Weeks passed before he was able to travel to the massacre site. When he finally arrived, he tried to retrace his previous steps to the place where he found the silver. He became disoriented, lost, and after an entire day of searching, was unable to find it.

There is an excellent chance that the silver remains at the lost location today. After a century-and-a-half, it is likely covered by a layer of soil. The possibilities of the silver being unearthed by a metal detector are excellent. If found today, it would be worth a fortune.

Penitentiary Treasure

An hour southwest of St. Louis is Washington County. That part of Missouri was the setting for an influx of settlers and farmers following the Civil War. In time, communities were established and families prospered. One such family was the Silveys. There are records that suggest the Silvey clan came from Tennessee. Other sources claim they migrated from Ohio. Whatever the truth, William Silvey lived just north of the tiny settlement of Shirley where he owned a prosperous farm and operated a general store.

William Silvey lived among citizens who were hard workers and provided adequately for their families. Given the economic situation of the times, Silvey was considered well-off, and from time to time his neighbors would approach him for a small loan. He always refused.

Like many during this time, Silvey harbored a distrust of banks. The tale that was told around Shirley at the time was that Silvey placed his money, all coins, in a metal bucket which he buried at some secret location. Silvey's wife tried to get him to reveal where the money was hidden in case anything happened to him, but he refused to tell her. He laughed at his wife's request, and told her he was going to outlive her by many years. The fewer people that knew about his treasure, he told her, the better.

By 1910, it was estimated that Silvey possessed a small fortune in silver coins in his bucket. Then, something happened that caused his fortune to be lost. William Silvey suffered a severe stroke.

During the days following his stroke, Silvey could do little but lie in bed. His movements were restricted and he had difficulty speaking, barely able to mouth a few words. His wife spoon-fed him broth and did what she could to make him comfortable. As the days wore on Silvey's condition worsened.

One day Mrs. Silvey asked her husband where he had hidden the family fortune. His eyes widened and he tried to speak, but could only sputter an unintelligible sound. For several days in a row he was asked the same question. Though Silvey tried to respond, he was unable. One day, his wife brought him a pencil and paper and attempted to get her husband to draw a map showing the location of the treasure. He was unable to control his hand.

Weeks passed, and every day Mrs. Silvey asked her husband the same question: where was the family fortune hidden? In time, Silvey regained a tiny amount of control over his speech. He was able to speak his wife's name and request water. Then, one morning when she asked him about the location of the bucketful of coins, he pointed out the window and spoke a word. Mrs. Silvey thought he said, "Penitentiary."

More time passed and Silvey's condition remained the same. And every morning when asked about the treasure he muttered the same word: penitentiary.

Mrs. Silvey was confused. As far as she knew there was no penitentiary in the area outside of one near St. Louis.

She knew that neither her husband, nor any of his or her relatives, had served time in a penitentiary. To her, his answer was meaningless.

William Silvey lingered for months and finally died. Unable to maintain the farm and run the general store, Mrs. Silvey moved from the area to live with relatives. It was not known where she went and she never returned to Washington County again.

In 1921, a young man arrived in Shirley. He identified himself as a relative of William Silvey's. Some recalled he was a son, others said he was a nephew. He said he had come in search of his father's fortune which had been hidden in some secret location on the family property.

The young relative spoke with several Shirley residents, but after a few days had learned little about where William Silvey might have hidden his treasure. Not a single person he spoke with could attach any meaning to the word "penitentiary."

The relative was about to abandon his quest for the treasure when he chanced upon an old man who lived alone one mile from Shirley. The old fellow told his visitor that he had known William Silvey, that he had traded in his general store at times. He described Silvey as being careful with his money, always counting out change two or three times to make certain he was not handing over too much. Silvey, according to the old man, was a bit of a miser.

When the visitor asked the old man if the word penitentiary meant anything to people in the area, he received a revealing response. The old man said that not far from the old Silvey farm was an unimpressive gorge eroded into the hills and known by only a few as Penitentiary Hollow. Through this narrow cut flowed a small stream called Penitentiary Creek.

That was it, thought the visitor. William Silvey had apparently buried his bucketful of silver coins at some location in Penitentiary Hollow. He asked for and received directions to the hollow. The next day he traveled to it.

Penitentiary Hollow was relatively short and narrow, but once there, the young man realized there were uncountable places where a bucket filled with coins could be buried. For two days he searched the hollow looking for a pertinent marker or some indicator of where Silvey's fortune was buried. He found nothing. *near IR to see path?*

It is alleged that William Silvey visited his treasure cache once every week or two, dug it up, and deposited the new coins taken during the course of his business operations. Thus, it is believed that the bucket would not be buried deep in the ground.

So little is known about Silvey's lost treasure that it is unlikely that many, or any, have traveled to Penitentiary Hollow to try to locate it. The chances that it still lies only a few inches below the surface are great, and the potential for finding it is high.

Immigrant Treasure

By the end of the second decade of the nineteenth century, a number of wagon routes from the east to a variety of western destinations had become well-established. As news of available farmland and settlement opportunities reached people living in the northern and eastern parts of the country, traffic along these routes increased.

As one story goes, in 1825 a party of immigrants departed from some location in central Pennsylvania bound for a California destination. The travelers pooled their savings, mostly in gold coins, and transported it in two metal boxes. The money was to be used to finance the trip across the continent and to assist them in beginning their new lives in California. Warned of bandits they might encounter along the trail, the travelers were advised to hide their money each night when they made camp. Every evening as the wagons were pulled into a circle, firewood was collected, and meals prepared, three men were assigned the job of selecting a suitable hiding place to bury the coins.

In addition to their personal possessions, the immigrants herded along two dozen cattle and several horses. The livestock represented their start on a collective farming operation once they arrived in California. The wagons were pulled by mules and oxen.

By summer, the immigrants arrived at the tiny community of Georgetown located along the wagon route in western Missouri and about sixty miles southeast of downtown Kansas City. Georgetown was one of many places wagon trains stopped during the journey westward. Firewood and fresh water was plentiful, and a small mercantile sold needed staples such as flour, corn meal, and coffee. Ammunition could also be purchased in Georgetown. Because Indian depredations were known to occur regularly to the west, travelers stocked up on bullets at the settlement.

The immigrants rested themselves and their stock near Georgetown for two days, then proceeded westward. Travel was slow. Recent rains had caused the ground to be soft and the wagons bogged down easily. Creeks were swollen such that the immigrants were forced to wait for hours before crossing. On the evening of the third day, they arrived at Big Walnut Creek. They crossed the creek with little difficulty and established the evening's campsite at the location called Twin Knobs. As was their habit, the gold-filled boxes were removed from the wagon bed and buried at a nearby location.

Unknown to the immigrants, a party of Osage Indians was camped a short distance away where Big Walnut Creek made a wide U-shaped bend. The Osage had spotted the travelers as they made the crossing. From the concealment of trees and brush, they observed the immigrants go about the business of setting up camp, preparing dinner, and caring for the livestock.

It was the livestock, particularly the horses, that caught the attention of the Indians. When the immigrants went to sleep for the night, they intended to sneak into the camp and steal the horses. Their plans were interrupted, however, when they saw that an armed guard was placed on the animals. They decided to wait until dawn to attack the camp.

The next morning as campfires were revived and the preparation of breakfast under way, the Osage launched a sudden assault on the immigrants. Every member of the wagon train was slain and the horses and mules driven off. Before departing the scene, the Indians set fire to all of the wagons. Months later, another wagon train arrived at Twin Knobs to set up camp. To their dismay, they found the ground littered with charred wood and metal fittings from the burned wagons. By this time, most of the remains of the burned wagon train had been washed away as a result of the frequent rains. Here and there at the campsite, the newcomers encountered skeletons of the earlier massacre. By 1829, according to historical records, little remained at Twin Knobs to suggest that a disaster had taken place.

It was not until 1873 that the origin, destination, and the identities of the Pennsylvania immigrants were learned. During this time, their practice of burying their gold at some secret location near camp every night was learned. Intrigued by such information, some hopeful treasure hunter would occasionally visit Twin Knobs to search for the gold. Items such as rusted wheel rims, bridle bits, and other metal items were found at a location a short distance north of Twin Knobs, a site that could have served as an excellent campsite. No trace of the gold was ever found.

Only a handful of people today know the tale of the massacred immigrants at Twin Knobs. As a result, few, if any, have endeavored to undertake a search for the buried gold-filled metal boxes. Given the sophistication of modern metal detecting equipment, the chances of locating the treasure could be good. It is likely buried only a few inches below the surface. Finding Twin Knobs should be easy. From there, locating a site where a wagon train full of people might set up a suitable camp would be the next step. In or near this area is where the gold would be found.

Near IR to find wagon trails?

The Ransom Treasure

In 1953, the nation was stunned at the news of the kidnapping and subsequent murder of six-year-old Bobby Greenlease. Young Greenlease was the son of a wealthy St. Louis family. On September 28, 1953 he was abducted. A ransom note demanding payment of $600,000 was left behind. It specified that it was to be paid with 20,000 twenty-dollar bills and 20,000 ten-dollar bills. The instructions were followed and the ransom paid, deposited at the location identified by the kidnappers. Following the payment of the ransom, nothing was heard from the kidnappers, and the Greenlease boy was never returned.

On November 3, Carl Hall and Bonnie Heady were arrested for the kidnapping and suspected murder of Bobby Greenlease. A short time later, the two led law enforcement authorities to a location where they had buried the slain child. During the arrest, approximately $290,000 of the ransom money was recovered. When Hall was interrogated about the remainder of the money, he related a story about caching it at a secret location.

Two days after receiving the ransom money, Hall went to a St. Louis hardware store and purchased a shovel and two garbage cans with lids. He carried his purchases to his quarters and loaded slightly more than $300,000 in small bills in the cans. He then rented an automobile, placed the money-filled cans and the shovel into the trunk, and drove to a motel located next to the nearby Meramec River. He checked into a room. Under the cover of a dark night, he dragged the two heavy garbage cans down to the bank of the river, excavated a large hole, and buried them. When pressed for details, Hall claimed that he had been under the influence of alcohol and drugs during the entire kidnapping and ransom ordeal and was unable to recall much of anything. He could not remember which motel he checked into. Subsequent investigation of the all of the motels along the Meramec River showed no one named Carl Hall had registered. Hall said he used a phony name but could not remember which one.

Hall was given several opportunities to take authorities to the location of the buried ransom money. It was rumored he would be offered a life sentence instead of the death penalty if he would reveal the location of the buried cans, but he was never able to provide the information. Up to the time Hall was executed for the kidnapping and murder of Bobby Greenlease, he stuck to his story about the buried money.

Hall's explanation has been verified in part. The owner of the hardware store where he obtained the garbage cans and shovel came forward with a record of the transaction. On at least two occasions, witnesses provided the information that they had observed a man wrestling two garbage cans down a bank toward the river. When pressed for details, however, neither of the witnesses could remember the exact location.

To date, the remaining Greenlease ransom money has not been found. Given the existing testimony, it is logical to assume it is exactly where Carl Hall said he buried it – at some location on a bank of the Meramec River. It would be a matter of some research to determine the locations of the motels located along that stretch of river in 1953.

There is another twist to this lost treasure story. The serial numbers of each of the bills used in the payment of the ransom were recorded by the Federal Bureau of Investigation. Technically, if the ransom treasure were found today it would have to be turned over to the authorities. This has deterred some professional treasure hunters from searching for the cache. However, there is some good news. The federal government is willing to pay a ten percent recovery fee if the ransom money is ever found.

If you enjoyed
LOST MINES AND BURIED TREASURES OF MISSOURI,
you'll love our other titles from author W.C. Jameson...

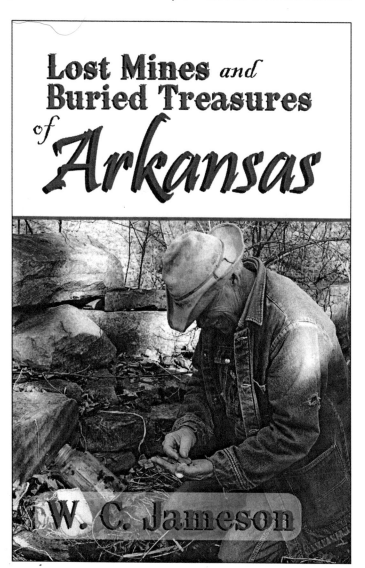

CPSIA information can be obtained at www.ICGtesting.com
Printed in the USA
LVOW13s2350290414

383805LV00001B/19/P